The Social Toddler

The Social Toddler

Helen and Clive Dorman

Consultant

Hilton Davis
Professor of Child Health Psychology
The Centre for Parent and Child Support, The Munro Centre, Guy's Hospital, London

Editor

Sue Parish

CP PUBLISHING

To our children, Charlie, Barney and Hannah

First published in 2002 by CP Publishing
an imprint of The Children's Project Ltd
PO Box 2, Richmond, Surrey, United Kingdom

www.childrensproject.co.uk
www.cpshopping.co.uk

Consultant, Hilton Davis
Professor of Child Health Psychology
The Centre for Parent and Child Support,
The Munro Centre, Guy's Hospital, London

Edited by Sue Parish
Designed by Clive Dorman

ISBN Paperback: 1 903275 38 5
ISBN Hardback: 1 903275 30 X

Printed and bound in Spain by Bookprint, S.L., Barcelona

CONTENTS

PREFACE

Children are fascinating. They have kept me occupied and profoundly interested for many years, both as a clinical psychologist concerned with finding ways to help them and their parents, and as a parent myself.

Although there are wonderful rewards, the task for parents is not easy. It takes considerable time and energy, involving a commitment like no other. At times, it might seem like a journey on which the risks of taking a wrong turning are very high, while following a path that is not well signposted, and to a destination that is entirely unclear.

It is not surprising, therefore, that there has been over many years a vast array of audacious people with ready advice, related more or less to an uncertain knowledge of developmental principles or to frameworks such as social learning theory. This has been dispensed largely through the written word, to those who are motivated to read, although more recently there has been a growing and valuable emphasis upon training courses.

However, gone are the days of thinking that there is a correct way to be a parent and that the outcomes are entirely in the adult's hands. Children come into the world as amazingly skilled individuals, building models of the world as they see it, with a powerful influence on the people around them. The essence, therefore, of the parenting task is to be able to adapt to children, work in partnership with them, understand their developing picture of the world and communicate effectively so as to meet their needs. The only vehicle for this is the relationship, initiated and sustained by a continual cycle of interaction. Parenting is by definition a social activity that requires a clear focus upon the child, sensitivity to the cues given through all aspects of their behaviour, and a clear understanding of what they mean, think, feel or need. This demands of parents many and varied qualities, but includes a genuine respect for and interest in the child, the strength to sustain this (fuelled by a support system) and, above all, empathy.

Empathy – defined as trying to understand the world from the viewpoint of the child – is the major focus of this book. Throughout my working life, I have looked for materials that might help students and parents truly understand children and how to interact with them. I have found many useful books, but none as good as *The Social Toddler*. It is unique in bringing the minds of children to life in a way that developmental texts do not. It attempts to give a realistic and useful insight into their thoughts and feelings, using pictures as much as words, showing sequences of behaviour in contexts, from which meaning can be inferred.

Although there are implications for parents' behaviour, the book avoids telling the reader what to do. Instead, it is highly successful in indicating something of what is going on in children's heads. At the very least it is stimulating, and motivates one to think about and to try to understand the child's point of view.

It can be read simply for the delightful charm of the children portrayed and their actions, but it is potentially much more useful. As a wonderful sequel to *The Social Baby*, which portrayed beautifully the nature of infants, this book dismisses the notion of toddlerhood as being simply a difficult period, and provides valuable insights into all aspects of children's behaviour. Although the authors provide interpretations throughout, they do so with humility. You will find many truths behind the behaviours, which I had fun thinking of and comparing alternatives – and simply attempting to understand. I enjoyed the process, learned a great deal from it, and I hope you do too.

HILTON DAVIS
Professor of Child Health Psychology
The Centre for Parent and Child Support,
The Munro Centre, Guy's Hospital, London

ACKNOWLEDGEMENTS

Certain people are key to our being able to write this book – some inspirationally, some practically and some emotionally. Right at the top of the list are the children we have worked with, each of whom is a gem, and their families; none more so than Sarah, Mark and Jake.

No book is the result of one or two individuals working in isolation, and in putting together *The Social Toddler* we have we have drawn upon the pioneering work of Mary Sheridan, Caroline Webster-Stratton, Donald Winnicott and T Berry Brazelton.

Special thanks to Isobel McGrory, for her support and introducing us to the work of some of the above, and without whom we would not have been able to view Hannah's life from her viewpoint; to Liz Andrews for teaching us a person-centred approach to babies and small children; to Hilton Davis, for his support and advice during the production of this book; to Penelope Leach for her practical comments; to Jonathan Hill for introducing us to Lynne Murray and her work on infant communication used in *The Social Baby;* to Andrea Sulley, Sally Jaeckle and Mary Fawcett from The Bristol Standard Birth to Three's working group; and to Sue Parish for reading the manuscript.

Some of the pictures in this book are from material produced for, or in association with: *The Social Baby* by Lynne Murray and Liz Andrews, The Children's Project, published 2000
The Bristol Standard
Parenting: parents and their babies, Liz Andrews and Julia Pemberton
Hannah is a big baby now! The Children's Project, published 2000
Milestones, The Children's Project, 2003

The following kindly assisted us with video filming:
Helen Zandbergs, Ellen and Rachel; Acorn Nursery, and St Richard's with St Andrew's Nursery, Richmond.
Tina Maberley; Ham Nursery, Richmond.
Hartcliffe, Highridge and Withywood Sure Start, Bristol.
Four Acres Family Unit and Nursery, Bristol
Amanda Rundle; Easton Community Centre, Bristol.
J Sainsbury PLC

Hilton Davis directs The Centre for Parent and Child Support (www.cpcs.org.uk). The Centre is based at The Munro Centre, Guy's Hospital and is part of the Child and Adolescent Mental Health Directorate of the South London and Maudsley NHS Trust. The Centre is supported by the charitable funds of Guy's and St Thomas' Hospitals and has close links with Kings College, University of London, via the Schools of Medicine and Nursing, and the Institute of Psychiatry. The Centre is able to offer consultation and advice to all agencies involved with the mental health of children, including health, education, social services and voluntary agencies. Contact: +44 (0)20 7378 3235 or linda.fone@kcl.ac.uk.
A new book from the centre: *Working in Partnership with Parents: the Parent Adviser Model* by Hilton Davis, Crispin Day and Christine Bidmead, The Psychological Corporation, published 2002.

Liz Andrews and Julia Pemberton run two- and three-day courses for health professionals on the practical application of the person-centered approach and infant social development, as presented in *The Social Baby.*

FOREWORD

The baby and childcare sections of shops and sites in the real world and in cyberspace are so crammed with books and magazines that it's difficult to distinguish one from another, let alone judge which will be enjoyable and which to believe. They are all written by experts (who keep stressing that they are also parents) or by parents (who stress that personal experience makes them experts too). They are almost all written exclusively for parents (as if nobody else takes care of children) and about problems, as if that is most of what children are.

This book is different, though. *The Social Toddler* was, of course, written and filmed and put together by adults (and yes, they are parents and parent-friendly experts). But it is as close as a book of serious adult intent can get to being created by toddlers and, in a sense, for toddlers too. The Dormans use their patiently observed and brilliantly photographed picture-stories to illuminate the mysteries of toddler thinking – thinking that make them so different from older children and therefore so hard to understand; to light up the dark corners of adult-toddler relationships where power struggles lurk, pretending to be 'discipline'; and to give visual-voice to feelings children cannot yet express for themselves and to questions they cannot ask.

Everyone knows that toddlers aren't babies any more, but are not yet children. But the fact that they are neither one of those things nor the other doesn't mean that they are nothing but in-betweens who should grow up into preschool children as fast as possible. Toddlerhood isn't just a tricky road to be hurried across. It's an important stage in children's development, with its own valid programme of growth and learning and change which cannot be compressed and should not be ignored. *The Social Toddler* sets out that programme, asking, on behalf of all toddlers, for adult understanding, patience and pleasure, and showing how rapidly these alone can transform apparently 'terrible two's' into terrific toddlers.

PENELOPE LEACH
Research Psychologist

Penelope Leach Ph.D is a research psychologist specialising in child development, and a passionate advocate for children and parents. She is president of the National Child Minding Association; a trustee of Home-Start; a founding committee member of the UK branch of the World Association for Infant Mental Health – and a mother and grandmother.

Penelope is best known for her world bestseller, *Your Baby and Child*

THE CHILDREN'S PROJECT AND *THE SOCIAL TODDLER*

Parenting is the single most demanding and time-consuming task we can take on, yet it is something we do without training. It is not until we have a sensitive or demanding child that we realise how little we really understand about our children.

Our daughter, Hannah, was born in 1993, a sensitive and active child. A close friend had worked as a psycho-social family-centred nurse, working with children therapeutically in the community, at the Cassel Hospital in Ham, and it was she who made us aware of a child-centred approach to parenting, and some of the reasons why Hannah might be behaving the way she was. Without her support and understanding, we may well have had a very different child from the one we have now. We had made a conscious decision to parent without smacking, but our experience made us realise how important it is for the well-being of all families to receive help and support right from the very start, and how easy it can be for us to slip into a negative cycle. We founded The Children's Project and began learning, researching and observing. We believe that by showing why children behave the way they do, parents and carers will be better able to understand them and respond appropriately. Our mission is to support preschool families and improve outcomes for children.

Whatever has gone before, there are clear signs in the West that our society is not developing in the way many of us want, or hope. Crime is on the increase, the misuse of drugs is becomming frighteningly commonplace, and we live with levels of disfunctional and antisocial behaviour that is beyond imagination. Often liberalisation is blamed for this, but we have to ask ourselves that, if this is true, why are get-tough policies, longer jail sentences and a growing prison population not deterring offenders?

We founded The Children's Project to try and address these issues: why is society becoming so fragile, and why are there so many angry and frustrated people out there?

We began by looking at what causes dysfunction and where it begins. It seems bizarre that people only get help once their level of dysfunction has reached such an extreme that they become unlawful, and are locked away. Society then attempts to rehabilitate the individual in the hope they can be released back into the community as a reformed person. In many cases this is true, but could not these people have been supported before, and the prison sentence avoided? Governments put money into youth support programmes, but is this not still too late?

School children are increasingly showing signs of antisocial behaviour and stress, but schools are under considerable pressure to deliver their educational programmes, and produce academic excellence. They are not resourced to support needy or challenging children other than with get-tough policies and exclusion. How does this support the child? Do we go back earlier? Some children starting nursery or primary school are considered difficult, or problem children; once labelled in this way, the child often faces lifelong exclusion and becomes increasingly angry.

So what makes some children so problematic? Is it bad parenting or is there another reason? If the child is someone else's then the finger often points at parenting. If it is our own child it's another reason – no-one understands what it's like. The difficulty is that our society labels or categorises children into groups: babies, toddlers, children and then teenagers. There are preconceptions about each of these groups, telling us what they do and how we should expect them to behave. This is largely connected to our expectation of how we behave as adults, and applying the same rules to children in order for them to learn. It wrongly assumes that all children are the same, and that if we are firm enough with them they will be compliant. This takes no account of individual differences. Adults are different and we celebrate and accept this. We would never compare a top athelete with an insurance underwriter, or a poet, yet many of the qualities that made each of them what they are were in place at birth: much of the rest is learned through experience.

So where does dysfunctional, or antisocial behaviour start? Some would say in the toddler years. In the West, we systematically and culturally demonise our children. We make comedy out of this; in books, on television and in films. It is funny to see a child behaving outrageously, as we mostly have had some experience of it; and generally having failed to resolve it, humour helps us feel better. In reality, we dread it. People say small children can be wilful, naughty, and spiteful; or that they do things deliberately to get at us, or just because they know they shouldn't. This is what we aim to address in this book.

The Social Toddler is not a 'how-to' parenting book, and it does not say to parents and carers how they should raise children. We show why children behave the way they do – and we hope, in some depth: with the benefit of this understanding, parents and carers can then apply their own standards and respond in a way that they feel is appropriate. To over simplify the point, if a child breaks his or her leg, we don't become cross with them because they cannot walk, or because they cry. We know they are not able, we understand and empathise. However, a great many of our expectations for young children are simply beyond their ability.

There are no quick fixes, or magic tricks for parents. It is just as demanding to be endlessly supportive, attentive and praising as it is to be in conflct. The difference is that children in conflict tend to continue in conflict throughout life, whereas supported children tend to become less demanding and more independent. The considerable effort put into the early years reaps enormous rewards from quite an early age.

Research both in the UK* and the USA has shown beyond question the enormous cost to society of dysfunctional or antisocial behaviour: in accidents and medical care, in damage to property, in crime, drink and drug abuse, in state benefits and providing prison accommodation: in breakdown of relationships, domestic violence and low academic achievement (poor readers). The cost is up to ten times that of a normally functioning family. It is estimated that the 12% of the population falling into this group account for half of public expenditure. It has further been shown that early intervention programmes for children aged 3–8 are significantly more effective than programmes for teenagers with serious antisocial behaviour. Parent training programmes typically cost £600 per child. To identify a young offender cost £3,700 in police and court costs. To then keep a teenager in a young offender's unit costs £3,500 *per week* (1998 figures). Common sense alone clearly makes social investment in early intervention a better option – as we say: '*Starting from day one to make the difference.*' Parenting should form part of our education in schools, and in antenatal classes.

Researching, writing and producing *The Social Toddler* has been an extraordinary experience. Being allowed to share people's lives with the added intrusion of video cameras has been both a humbling experience, and an honour. It is fascinating that on some occasions we would leave a family unsure of the value of what we had filmed. It was only when we were able to look at the material in depth, and slow it down, that the true beauty of the children's behaviour was revealed. Of course, it is impossible to observe our children in such depth all the time, and we should not expect to, but by taking a step back, and trying to see our children's actions from their viewpoint, we can make our relationships with them exciting, enjoyable, and so much more rewarding.

HELEN AND CLIVE DORMAN
Directors and Co-founders, The Children's Project

* Source and references BMJ vol. 323, pp191, 194, 28 July 2001. Full text, web: www.bmj.com

INTRODUCTION

WHO ARE WE?

Humans are one of the most complex species on the planet. The simple fact that we have the ability to think, reason, solve problems and communicate our thoughts sets us apart from other animals and enables us to understand a lot about the world in which we live. We appreciate the concept of time – past, present and future; and we know that there is a cycle of life – we are born, we grow and we die. We know that eating, drinking and sleep are our basic needs and that reproduction is fundamental to the survival and future of our species: and we know that the future of our species is the one thing we can influence by the way in which we raise and educate our children.

Regardless of culture, race, religion or gender, much of what we do as humans is common across these boundaries: the image of ourselves we portray to others in 'our world' is very important to us; the clothes we wear, the style of our hair, the car we drive, even the sort of language we use, says a lot about us to the

people we meet. We know exactly what we like and dislike about our appearance and, consciously or not, we spend a considerable amount of time and effort on self image. We do this to help us feel we are part of a community and to create a sense of belonging, and we change our appearance to suit different places and activities, for example in work and at leisure. When we look at ourselves in a mirror we see our own perception of our image and identity, and where we are placed in 'our world'. We may not always be content with what we see – which is part of what makes us who we are – but we do have a good idea of what we would like to be and what we want from life and those around us. However, we rarely stop to think how we arrived at this point, or consider that it could be anything other than our own conscious choice. A great deal of how we perceive ourselves and the world around us is directly linked to our childhood experiences. To really see how our image and identity was created we need to take a step back, look into our minds and try to understand what has made each of us into the unique, independent-thinking, reasoning and problem-solving adult we are today.

On a daily basis we carry out routine tasks without much thought. We do this automatically and often perform a number of them at the same time; for example, washing up and listening to the radio, whilst planning for a meeting or an outing the following day, represents an amazing range of mental and physical skills which we have come to take for granted. It's only when we are presented with a new task and we are forced to use our powers of concentration that we stop and think about what we are doing. Once learned, and if repeated frequently, the new task quickly ceases to be a challenge and becomes easy and automatic. For example, do you remember your first driving lesson or your first introduction to a computer and attempts to access the internet, and how daunting you found it? The experts seem to make it all look so easy which in turn probably made you feel completely hopeless. Would you ever be as good as them? How did that make you feel – like giving up, or more determined to succeed? These examples give us an insight into what our young children experience every single day as they struggle to learn and understand what to us, 'the experts', are the simplest of tasks.

Much of what children do is a response to what we adults say or ask of them in relation to their perception of 'their world'. Their world is a very different place from ours: it is governed by the stages of development of the brain and the child's physical and mental ability, in the context of their day-to-day experiences, which are all closely linked. In order truly to understand our young children we need to know a little about how the human brain develops and what makes it tick. We also need to revert back to childhood and remember our own experiences in order to try and see life from a child's perspective.

A LITTLE ABOUT THE HUMAN BRAIN

For a developing child, the human brain is the most important organ of the body; a large 'biological plasticised computer' that is able to change constantly, adapt to any input, and continually reorganise itself to accommodate changing circumstances as we progress through our journey of life. The brain controls every single thing we do – our bodily functions through the central nervous system and all areas of our development; movement and co-ordination, emotions, self-esteem, thinking, learning, self-control, perception (including the five senses, sight, hearing, touch, smell and taste), and language.

In recent years, understanding of how the brain develops has increased enormously. Much research has been carried out and, whilst we are still learning, we know a great deal more about what happens to the brain in the early years.

The brain is made up in part of what is in our genes and inherited – our physical appearance and fundamental personality – about which there is little we can do. The rest of our character is influenced by daily experiences from birth in 'our world', making each of our brains function differently, and influencing how our children's brains will develop.

HOW THE BRAIN DEVELOPS

The brain works by sending electrical signals between brain cells (neurons). To do this it needs energy in the form of glucose, which it burns. A baby is born with all the brain cells he or she will have in her lifetime – some one hundred billion of them. At birth they are not all fully connected, but as a child grows and experiences what is 'their world', the brain makes connections between cells in order to send signals, which become paths of communication (known as synapses). Each cell is capable of having multiple connections with other cells – and the permutations are virtually limitless. Any experience helps form these connections and, during the first three years, the brain makes synapses at a remarkable rate – more than twice as many as will remain through to adulthood. During the first three years, the brain makes over one thousand trillion connections between cells. This means that the pre-school child's brain is more connected and flexible than that of any adult, and therefore it is far more receptive to receiving information and learning. However, the brain continually 'rewires' itself as it adjusts to changes in experience, reinforcing frequently used synapses, and severing unused ones.

So, repetition in the early years, both good and bad, will strengthen the synapses that respond to that experience, affecting how the brain develops and the outcome for the child. Up to the age of ten the brain is twice as active as an adult's, and by the age of ten many of the most active synapses have become permanently connected and will be retained for life; but other less used ones will disappear. The brain is highly efficient with itself and from time to time will have a 'spring clean', ruthlessly clearing out little-used paths. Many little-used cells that were present at birth will die. This 'springclean' of the brain happens naturally, and as the brain matures, different parts of the brain specialise in different functions.

In an adult there are literally billions of connections in the brain, a response to a lifetime's experience that makes each of us the unique individual we are. It is the natural way for a human brain to develop and it is a process that continues throughout adult life – something that enables an adult to learn something new, and learn to be different.

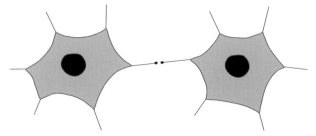

HOW THE CHILD DEVELOPS

Of course, the brain is not a mass of disorganised cells waiting for an experience in order to get connected. Different parts of the brain look after different functions, and from birth it controls the development of the child in a very logical way.

There are three areas of development:

Physical development

This is how the body grows and the increasing ability to control movements. Muscles and bones, height, weight, health and eating all come into this group. The ability to move and control parts of the body, called motor skills, is divided into large movements (learning to throw, catch, run and jump), and small movements (learning to draw, or tie shoe laces).

Mental (or cognitive) development

The dictionary definition of cognitive is: *connected with thinking or conscious mental processes*. It is the extent of our ability to do this that makes the human species unique and that sets us apart from other animals – to think and reason; use memory, perception and imagination; process information, solve problems, learn and use language. This also includes how we interpret the five senses: sight, hearing, touch, smell and taste.

Social and emotional development

This is the development of emotions, personality, self-esteem and, importantly, communication. This enables relationships to develop between the child and other people – children, peers, and developing attachments with adults. It is how children move from being totally dependent to being increasingly independent; and how they work, play, accept rules, and learn to trust others. Children can use their senses and emotions to decide what they like or do not like, what they are happy with or not. As the brain develops they are better able to make sense of their feelings and relate them to what is happening around them, and convey this to others. They also become better at thinking and remembering.

Although the physical, mental and emotional areas develop at the same time, they do not all develop at the same speed. A child may be seen to progress in one area but then slow down in another. For example, whilst the brain concentrates on physical development – such as learning to stand or walk, it may slow down on mental development – language. This can be observed when friends with children of a similar age and development meet. There will be times when one child becomes much more mobile than the other, but his or her speech does not progress. The other child may well be using more words, but remain less mobile. In time, these differences even out and have little or no bearing on future outcome.

However, the three areas do influence one another and something learned in one will be applied to improve development in another. For example, using an object such as a chair to pull themselves up to a standing position is physical development; but once standing, the child will be able to see more, reach more and have access to a wider environment. From this, they learn that using an object to pull themselves up is a good way to get something that was previously out of reach – a step towards independence – which is both mental and emotional development.

A child's brain has its own inbuilt clock, programmed to develop the three areas at the optimum pace for the individual's own set of circumstances. This will differ from child to child and be influenced by experience, which is part of what makes every child unique. Parents and carers who are sensitive to their child's specific needs, and who support and encourage them to try and repeat new things, will be giving them a good start in life. Ignoring a child's natural pace or pushing them to try and achieve a goal before they are naturally ready can be harmful and, in some cases, can even produce the opposite result.

LOOKING BACK AT OUR OWN CHILDHOOD AND OURSELVES

We all know that we were once babies, but we have only sketchy memories of our very early years, if any at all. As babies we have limited conscious memory, something which develops as we get older, so it is likely that we will not remember a great deal about our early years, but can recall more about our later experiences as children. The brain strips out much of our early conscious memory during its process of development and refinement (of synapses).

Many of our parents brought us up with knowledge that has been handed down from generation to generation, and some old wives tales prevail today as sound advice. But to what extent has this influenced us? The event referred to in the phrase *'Look at me, it didn't do me any harm'*, often said with a wry smile, may well have had a significant effect on how we view our own role as a parent. There is growing evidence to suggest that in making decisions as a parent we draw upon our own very early experience – concious or otherwise, and that many of the foundations for parenting are laid down in the first three years, even after making allowances for individual temperament. If our own childhood experiences have been particularly negative, this can lead us to have negative feelings about our own parenting abilities. Whilst science and technology has progressed immeasurably over the decades, it seems many of our attitudes to how we raise young children have not. Society offers us so much opportunity to learn and improve, but our most important skill – parenting – has until recently been sadly neglected.

We all have widely differing circumstances and it is generally assumed that being a single parent – female or male, living in poor housing, unemployed or on low income puts an enormous strain upon parents' ability to parent. But equally, it is highly significant that modern work patterns have resulted in many couples re-locating to pursue work or their careers, and when the time comes to start a family the couple may find themselves miles away from other family members and friends. The couple's new family unit can also be separated, with husbands or partners working long hours away from home, and mothers at home for long periods, often for the first

time. Mothers who have previously worked may feel vulnerable at this time, and without support, both parents can end up feeling unsure and isolated, and unable to cope with the growing needs of a small child in our pressured society.

We would all love to have the best relationship with our children and enjoy their company, but frequently we are unable to. Babies and small children are endlessly demanding, with a relentless drive for repetition, to explore and discover. Sometimes we cannot see the good in our children and have negative feelings towards them simply because we are too tired and stressed living our modern lives; or we can't understand them and what they do doesn't make sense to us; or because of our own negative childhood experiences.

If we start by thinking about ourselves and try to build a picture of our own early experiences, we can begin to understand some of our past, reflect on this, and learn something about our own vulnerabilities so that we can see ahead more clearly.

It is important to remember that we can all learn to be different, and having negative feelings about our children, or our ability to be a parent, does not have to mean there is nothing that can be done – or that we are a bad parent. As humans, none of us are perfect; there will always be times when we get angry, frustrated or depressed, and most of us feel guilty when we say or do something we regret, but if we are able, we can learn about ourselves from these experiences. We can become better equipped to cope with our emotional responses, develop better self-control, and a more positive attitude to those around us, especially our children.

We should also never underestimate the effect that having a baby can have on us. For many years our only concern had been ourselves alone; then, for some time there were two, a couple who chose to be together. Now, suddenly there has been a life-changing experience and there are three or more unique individuals, each

with their own needs and demands, and all vying for attention. The birth experience, and the emotional and hormonal upheaval, can lead to many thoughts and feelings, both positive and negative. The expectation of childbirth can be very different from the reality and adjusting to this new situation can cause problems.

Following the birth it is likely that mother and baby will be together 24 hours a day, 7 days a week. Fathers too are being encouraged to spend more time with their new family, as more employers offer paternity as well as maternity leave. Having a baby is similar to meeting someone new and getting to know them. Sometimes we get on instantly and other times it is a far more gradual process.

If all of this is devastating, it's just the start of parenting. It is something we enter into with almost no training or prior knowledge. Nobody would expect anyone to teach our children in school without any training. But we are teachers for our children, and we are expected to be parents with no training, with minimal support and to be responsible should anything go wrong. It is never as easy as we think, particularly with our own child and especially if that child is demanding, or sensitive. As parents, we all do the best we can with the knowledge we have, but an understanding of *why* our children do the things they do, can be of help.

THE STORY SO FAR: THE FIRST YEAR

Even in the womb, babies are gaining a sense of the world into which they will be born. Babies will have become familiar with the everyday routine of their mother and the sounds they hear, including speech, and they can recognise the sound of their mother's voice, as well as those close to her. A baby is born with a wide range of basic human emotions such as pleasure, sadness, interest, fear and disgust, but the more complex emotions such as envy, guilt, embarrassment or hatred are learned through experience. Following a straightforward birth without too much medication, a newborn baby may often be awake for some hours. During this time the baby will be very interested in his or her surroundings, listening and actively showing great interest in human faces. New babies can focus up to approximately 23cm – the distance they will be from their mother's face during breast feeding; they can locate and turn to the sound of their mother's voice, even in a room with other voices; they will choose to look at a face shape in preference to a non-face shape, and can even copy facial expressions! Within hours babies prefer their mother's smell, made familiar from the taste of the amniotic fluid in the womb. Babies are drawn to high contrast images and can track a brightly coloured object or one that makes a noise.

Babies are born with primary reflexes: rooting and sucking; the ability to grasp a finger and curl toes in a grasping action; if held in a standing position with the feet placed on a hard surface, the legs will stiffen and make walking movements; in reaction to a sudden noise or touch, the arms will shoot out in a circular movement with the fingers splayed (the Moro reflex).

Whilst new babies clearly have remarkable abilities, there is much about which they have no concept. They do not yet know that they have a mind and believe everyone and everything is part of their world, so if one baby cries, another nearby will often start to cry as well. They are born with no sense of self and have no idea if they are a boy or a girl; no concept of being alive or dying. If they cannot see or hear something, it doesn't exist, and if they can see or hear something which then goes away, it ceases to exist. This is why babies will crumple into tears when their mother leaves the room – even for a moment. Before birth, babies begin to learn about their environment through experience rather than thought, thus building a sense of their world, and their place in it. Babies have a natural instinct to feed and sleep, plus a strong desire for human contact, social interaction and stimulation, so how

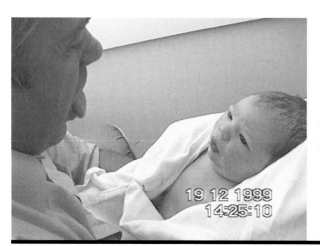

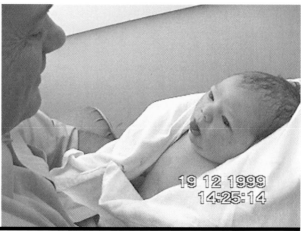

1 Ethan is 18 minutes old. He studies his father's face as John protudes his tongue.

2 A few seconds later, Ethan protrudes his own tongue. *(Pictures taken from* The Social Baby.*)*

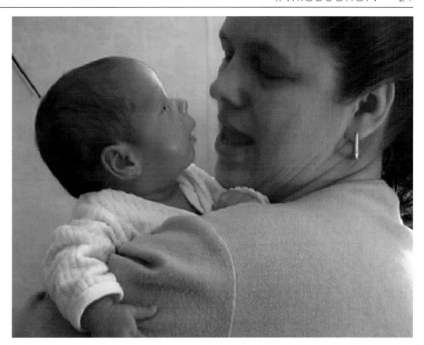

At two weeks old, Asher makes a great effort to raise his head and engage with his mother, Bethan. He is clearly looking and listening as she talks to him.

we respond and interact with babies helps them to feel secure or otherwise in their world – and will influence the development of patterns of behaviour.

During the first year, babies undergo remarkable changes physically, mentally and socially. The physical change is the more obvious as seemingly involuntary movements become more purposeful and accurate. Initially restricted to lying on their backs, increasing strength in the baby's muscles enables them to roll over, sit up, crawl, pull themselves up and perhaps even walk – all within the first 12 months. Improving dexterity enables a baby to pick up and explore a variety of objects; learning more about what they can and cannot do also enhances communication skills. Socially, babies start to recognise familiar people and they soon develop a strong bond with those who are closest – their prime carer and a number of other people. This ability to form close bonds with more than one person is reassuring for parents who have to return to work. It also highlights the importance of quality and consistent child care.

As mobility improves, there is an increase in independence, but around the age of 6 months anything new or unfamiliar, including people, causes uncertainty. Babies rely upon their carers for reassurance, support and guidance to help them learn what may be safe or dangerous. This is why a baby that has previously smiled happily at everyone suddenly cries when she meets new people or those she has not seen frequently.

Mentally, there are the beginnings of an awareness of 'self', but babies will not be able to recognise their own 'self' as a reflected image in a mirror before they reach the age of 1½–2yrs. Babies have limited memories so they need to repeat actions frequently if they are to be stored by the brain. They also learn by trial and error, and cause and effect, which encourages the use of something we adults take for granted – thought. By applying thought processes they discover the differences between movements that are mechanical and those that are biological, showing a preference for the latter by the end of the first year. They also start to distinguish between what is living and what is non-living.

If we consider the changes from conception to birth, and through to the end of the first year, we can appreciate just how rapidly babies change physically, mentally and socially. They have a long way to go before they are independent people but they are making good progress so far.

LOOKING FORWARD TO WHAT IS AHEAD

Having seen how remarkable a baby's first year has been, we can look at the next phase of a baby's life and start to prepare for what is ahead, seeing why certain things occur and why certain things don't. One of the most difficult areas for parents to understand and tackle is that of coping with behaviour. We each have individual rules, based on our own standards and family values. These can sometimes differ quite widely between partners and no matter how difficult it may seem, it is vital that from the outset, all parties within the family unit discuss and agree to a common set of rules – rules that can be adhered to and which reflect both parents, even if they seem hard to keep. In time, children become excellent negotiators and learn how to get the best from their parents' inconsistencies.

Parents' expectations for their children will always be high. After all, it is natural to want your child to shine above the others and to be like you – with all your strengths but none of your weaknesses.

As the child grows and signs of independence begin to emerge, some of our expectations may turn to disappointment as behaviour patterns that weren't expected become apparent. At this point it may be worth reflecting on our own 'perfection' and whether we would want to live with ourselves! Relationships and friendships are a partnership, built on trust, over time' respecting one another as individuals, allowing one another personal space, sharing feelings and experiences, and, just as important, admitting our own faults and weakness – being able to say we were wrong and that we are sorry.

We are all unique and so are our children, therefore we cannot make them into something they are not. A child inherits certain personality traits through the parents' genes, but the way a child grows up and develops depends on what the child experiences; we as parents and our parenting skills play a key role in this.

Everything changes when we have children and any event can become a treasured moment.

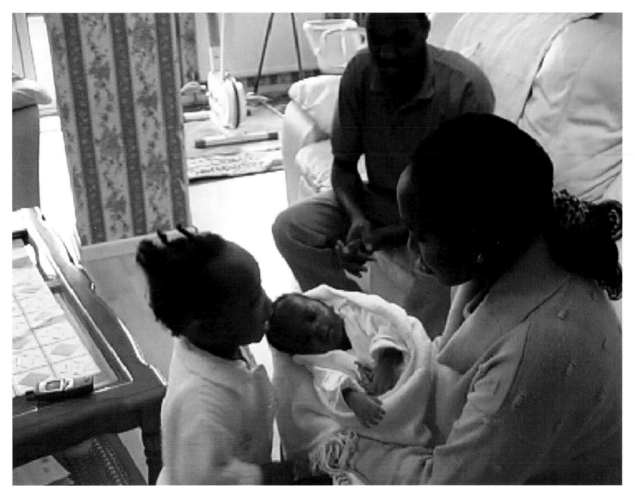

SECTION ONE

PARENTING FROM

A CHILD'S VIEWPOINT

🎥 *Picture story*

A CHILD'S EYE VIEW

When we are out shopping we focus on the task in hand and barely notice our surroundings unless there is a significant change, such as a new window display.

For a small child, however, much of this is a new and very stimulating experience. The brain needs to process the sights, sounds and smells the child takes in, connect them together and begin to try and make some sense of it all. A small child can learn a lot by simply going in a buggy for a short outing.

To help get a better idea of what small children see from their perspective – that is, close to the ground – we shot some film as if we were aged about 12 months old and were sitting in a buggy.

WE MAY BE ADULTS BUT WE CAN STILL PRETEND (1)

Empathy: *the ability to share someone else's feelings or experiences by imagining what it would be like to be in their situation.*

The essence of parenting is to listen, and by listening we can learn to empathise.

No adult can fully understand what it is really like to be a child: we have become too sophisticated, though occasionally we get a taste of it when asked to learn a new skill, as mentioned previously. But what we *can* do is pretend to be a child again and experience what it is like for them. This will give us an insight into a child's world and help us empathise with our children.

A child's physical and mental abilities develop rapidly during the preschool years, but the basic need for love, guidance and boundaries remain the same throughout their childhood. Awareness and sensitivity in certain situations will help prevent potential conflicts; support and nurture will benefit the child and be very rewarding for parents.

WHAT'S IT LIKE TO BE A SMALL PERSON?

With Helen (H) in the role of a parent, Natalia (N) and Sarah (S) were asked to role-play a variety of situations to demonstrate how we use language and actions in our day-to-day lives, and then to report their feelings. (For this exercise we assumed N and S, when playing children, could understand all that was being said).

2 Sarah looks up at Helen.
S: *'It's quite daunting.'*

2 A PARENT ENGROSSED IN TALKING TO A FRIEND

Sarah has been asked to get Helen's attention without speaking.

1 Sarah pulls at Helen's clothes; she also tried to bite, thought about running off and finally screamed.

1 DIFFERENCE IN HEIGHT

Having someone tower over us is quite intimidating.

1 S: *'Normally I have conversations with adults like this.'*

THE CHILD'S VIEWPOINT

3 Helen demonstrates an aggressive action to Sarah, who backs off and says, *'No, I don't like that.'*

4 H: *If I come down to your eye level, how does that feel?*
S: *'More relaxed, more comfortable, definitely.'*

2 S: *'That's so frustrating, annoying; you're winding me up even more. It's not nice.'*

THE CHILD'S VIEWPOINT

Young children find it very hard to wait for anything; they live for 'now' and have no concept of time. With limited communication skills, children resort to whatever means they can to get our attention.

Parents can take a break in the conversation, attend to the child's need and then either continue the conversation or arrange to speak another time.

continues overleaf...

WE MAY BE ADULTS BUT WE CAN STILL PRETEND (2)

continued from previous page

3 TALKING ABOUT A CHILD IN A CRITICAL WAY

1 Helen is talking to Natalia about Sarah. She complains about how useless Sarah is when she compares her with other children who are more accomplished.

4 UNREALISTIC EXPECTATIONS

1 H: *'Go on, Natalia, sing that song for Sarah, like you did for me.'*

5 TOO MANY INSTRUCTIONS AT ONCE

Helen gives Sarah a number of complex instructions to follow, much the same as we would when giving directions.

1 Sarah concentrates as Helen delivers instructions one after the other.

THE CHILD'S VIEWPOINT

When a child is quiet we often forget they are there – as Natalia points out, *'We don't see our children'*, so it is important to think about what we say.

Children understand more than they can say. To run a child down by calling them 'an idiot' or 'stupid' is very hurtful, as Sarah found out.

2 Helen gives Sarah a hug after Sarah says how she felt. S: *'I'm standing here with the biggest frown on my face. I'd hate that.'*

THE CHILD'S VIEWPOINT

Some children are outgoing and some are shy. It is unrealistic to say to a shy child *'Go on, off you go and join in'* or expect them to perform like a child who is confident. Likewise to expect a fidgety child to sit for too long.

Natalia's reaction, *'I'd hate that, I'd really not want to do it.'*

2 Natalia doesn't want to, but Helen insists, pushing her forward while Sarah encourages, saying, *'Oh, go on.'*

THE CHILD'S VIEWPOINT

Children have short memories and attention spans. Give instructions one at a time, check they have understood, help and praise effort and/or success.

2 H: *'Off you go.'* Sarah closes her eyes to try to recall the order.

3 S: *'I can only remember the first two!'*

continues overleaf...

WE MAY BE ADULTS, BUT WE CAN STILL PRETEND (3)

continued from previous pages

6 USE OF LANGUAGE

Helen asks Sarah 'Go and hang your coat on the flandingo.'

1 H: *'...go on, off you go.'*
S: *'I don't even know what that is.'*

3 She then directs Sarah *'The flandingo, it's over there by the mirror.'*

7 FOOD ISSUES

Sarah is given cold beans to eat and Natalia is given finger foods.

1 Helen tries to make Sarah eat the cold beans which she hates, S: *'No way.'*

THE CHILD'S VIEWPOINT

Children are not always familar with words and concepts that we adults take for granted. Because we use them frequently, we wrongly assume children have understood and then wonder why they haven't complied with our request.

With help, children will learn and be able to carry them out successfully.

2 Here, Helen gives the instruction and waits to see if Sarah has understood.

4 Sarah looks round for reassurance, H: *'That's it, well done.'*

5 Helen gives Sarah a hug. S: *'I feel much better.'*

THE CHILD'S VIEWPOINT

Eating is a social and pleasurable event and children can learn a lot from food.

Pressure from parents to get their children to eat can give rise to food battles. Children are eager to copy their parents and feed themselves even if it means getting messy. Small amounts and a spoon or sliced finger foods are ideal.

2 Helen gets Natalia interested in the choice of finger foods she has been offered to eat.

continues overleaf...

WE MAY BE ADULTS, BUT WE CAN STILL PRETEND (4)

continued from previous pages

8 EYE-TO-EYE CONTACT

Natalia tries to get Helen to make eye contact with her and Helen tries to avoid her gaze.

1 Natalia talks to Helen, who avoids having eye contact with Natalia when they are speaking together.

9 PHYSICAL CONTACT

Physical contact is essential for human well-being.

THE CHILD'S VIEWPOINT

Hugging and touching gives children a sense of approval from their parents, and shows them they are wanted and cared for.

1 Helen puts her hands on Sarah as she speaks to her...

2 ...then they hug. S: *'Ah, that's nice.'*

11 TAKING OVER DURING PLAY

Sarah is playing happily with the dough. Helen decides that Sarah is not playing with the dough 'properly' and intervenes.

1 H: *'Sarah, that's wrong, you do it like this... no, not that shape, use this one.'*

THE CHILD'S VIEWPOINT

A baby is born with a preference for human contact, the face being of particular interest and where the baby's gaze is spent the longest.

Eye contact enhances bonding and a sense of belonging.

Parents who feel uncomfortable making eye-to-eye contact with adults may feel the same with their children.

For the child, an adult who is speaking, but not looking at them, can be forgiven for thinking he or she is not being spoken to.

2 Helen explains the importance of making eye-to-eye contact with other adults.

10 INTERFERING

Sarah and Natalia begin to draw and colour.

THE CHILD'S VIEWPOINT

Children need the freedom to express themselves in any way they feel. It really doesn't matter if a child paints the sun green or an elephant with stripes. Most adults have lost this ability and believe the image they produce has to be a perfect representation —
'Oh, I'm hopeless at drawing.'

1 Sarah chooses a crayon to colour in the fish she has drawn.

2 Helen comes over and says, 'No Sarah, fishes aren't that colour...'

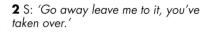

THE CHILD'S VIEWPOINT

Any type of play is good, as long as it is safe. Much of children's play may appear random and may make no sense to us but it is important to let children experiment and learn from their own creative play. If they need help, let them come to us first.

2 S: 'Go away leave me to it, you've taken over.'

3 Sarah plays happily again.

continues overleaf...

WE MAY BE ADULTS, BUT WE CAN STILL PRETEND (5)

continued from previous pages

12 GIVING WARNING

Sarah and Natalia enjoy playing with the dough.

1 Sarah and Natalia chat together as they play.

13 APPRECIATION

Natalia has just finished a drawing, with which she is very pleased.

1 Natalia beams as she shows Helen her picture, which she takes…

THE CHILD'S VIEWPOINT

Just as we do, children like their work to be appreciated. Whilst we may not understand what our children have drawn, it offers an ideal opportunity to praise them. By asking questions and showing interest we can gain an insight into 'their world'.

THE CHILD'S VIEWPOINT

Children have no concept of time and become absorbed in what they are doing. A warning that the activity is soon to end gives the child a chance to prepare.

2 Suddenly Helen dives in, gets hold of Natalia and tries to drag her away, *'Come on, we're going now.'* N: *'No way...'*

3 Helen warns Natalia they will soon have to leave, H: *'When you have finished that animal we are going.'* She may also need to help Natalia to end the activity before they leave.

2 ...and says *'Lovely dear.'* Helen walks off, showing that she is not really interested.

3 Natalia is left speechless: *'I don't know what to say.'*

4 H: *'Hey, Natalia that's brilliant, well done.'*

5 H: *'Is this your house?'*
N: *'No it's my auntie's, and these are the eyes...'*

HOW WE USE LANGUAGE

LISTENING AND SPEAKING CLEARLY

On the previous pages we have been able get an idea of what it is like to be a small child and how our actions can impact on them. Here we look at ways to communicate more clearly with our children and how to put this into practice. This is not a set of rules, or step-by-step instructions, but some general principles on which to lay the foundations for enhanced parenting skills.

Children learn a great deal from observation and repetition, and they will mimic the behaviour of those around them. As parents are a major influence in this, it is logical to assume that being positive and confident in what we do and say will be the most successful strategy in raising our children.

The way we use language is an important aspect of parenting. Children instinctively seek the approval of their parents: it is innate and in their own interest; but when we talk to a child we often use language that is complex and ambiguous, which we assume they can understand. This makes it very difficult for them to comply with what we have said, and despite their efforts we sometimes become irritated by what we see as their non-compliance. We need to learn to use language clearly and make it easy to understand. When we meet someone who speaks a foreign language we automatically speak differently, taking care to use clear, short, simple statements. Why not then for our children? Probably because we feel self-conscious, but it is a positive step towards getting a better response.

THE IMPORTANCE OF LISTENING

Listening is two-way and in order to get children to listen to us, we need to listen to them. Children who have limited language skills may not be able to convey clearly what they need. Listening, watching and interpreting their words and gestures, then saying what we think they mean or need first, will help two-way communication.

🎥 *Picture story*

MISUNDERSTANDINGS (1)

TOM *19 months*

Tom's mother, Mandy, misunderstands what he wants to do, which makes Tom very frustrated.

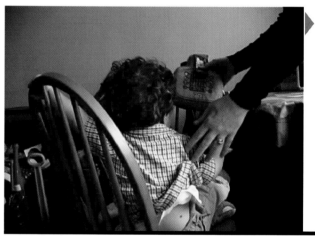

3 Mandy shows Tom the phone...

6 ...he looks up to Mandy for help, who misunderstands and asks, *'Do you want to get down?'*

1 Tom looks to Mandy who has placed a toy phone on the table. She presses it and it starts to 'talk'. He vocalises his need to get onto the chair.

2 Mandy helps Tom up onto the chair.

4 …which he indicates he wants on the table.

5 Tom begins to play happily, pressing the buttons, but the phone does not 'talk' …

7 Tom looks down at the ground… which Mandy takes as confirmation.

8 As Mandy lifts Tom from the chair, he vocalises loudly and shows his frustration, leaving her in no doubt that this time she has misinterpreted his expectation.

RESPECT AND POLITENESS IS TWO-WAY

We all expect a great deal of our children, and there is something charming about a polite small child. Much of a child's behaviour is based on experience, so let's look at some basics:

FIRST **STEP**s

- Children's first teachers are their parents

- By showing respect and politeness to children they will learn these vital social skills from an early age and will reciprocate

S – SORRY
T – THANK YOU
E – EXCUSE ME
P – PLEASE

- To admit to being wrong and to say sorry is not a fault or weakness, but a sign of great personal strength

- Small children do not yet know the concept of what's right and wrong, but when this has been learned, they will be better able to say sorry

- By learning these simple skills our children will be better equipped for life's ups and downs

---

POINTS TO CONSIDER WHEN GIVING INSTRUCTIONS

- Go to where the child is before you speak, to avoid shouting from a different place.

- Use the child's name to get his or her attention.

- Make sure the child is not absorbed in something else and is listening to what you are saying.

- When possible, get down to his or her eye level.

- Try to maintain a calm, steady, even tone of voice.

- Give a polite, clear, straightforward, attainable, non-critical, positive instruction so the child knows what is expected.

◉◉ ⬛ *Picture story*

MISUNDERSTANDINGS (2)

JAKE *24 months*

Jake's mother, Sarah, asks him to get a piece of rail track, but she has not got Jake's full attention. Although she helps him as much as she can, Jake shows he has remembered only the last few words that she spoke.

Getting children's attention

- Children are often completely engrossed in what they are doing and either do not hear you, or choose not to (*see 'Ignoring and going deaf', page 160*). Make sure the child is listening before you speak to them.

- Expect to repeat requests several times; if you find this difficult, count to ten to give the child a chance to react, and for you to remain calm.

- Give one instruction at a time, and when that has been completed, praise the child before giving the next instruction.

Make instructions attainable

Young children have short memories, they are easily distracted and sometimes find our use of language difficult to interpret. Make instructions realistic for the child's age. If the task has been accomplished successfully, praise should be given; if the child doesn't quite manage it this time, praise should still be given for the effort put in and to encourage for next time. Perhaps re-assess the instruction to see if it was too difficult to achieve in the first place.

Praising achievements

Children love to have the approval of adults. Praise them for any small achievement and the steps towards that achievement. Praising builds

1 Sarah directs Jake towards the toys as she asks him to go and get a piece of rail track. Jake looks in the direction in which Sarah is pointing.

2 Sarah helps by saying, *'Down there see, by the ball.'* Jake is looking at a favourite toy he is carrying...

3 ...and says *'Yes'* as he goes towards the rail track, but picks up the ball instead.

self-esteem, and will encourage them to try something new, confident that they will succeed in time.

Praise positives, ignore negatives

Always see the good in a child. Say *'Well done, good girl (or good boy),'* as often as you can. This may feel excessive, but a child quickly learns from this. Children prefer to do things that get a positive reponse. Ignore what goes wrong and give positive encouragement for them to repeat and succeed with the activity.

Say what you mean (children are very literal)

'Sally, put the toys away please' is a clear, direct instruction.

'You haven't put those toys away' is an observation. Do you want the toys put away? It is confusing and critical.

'Let's put the toys away' is OK if you intend to help, but confusing for your child if you don't.

Using 'do' words first, not 'don't' words

'Tom, don't run' doesn't make it clear what you want Tom to do.

'Tom, walk – thank you' means don't run and is a clear instruction.

Questions are OK if you give the right choice

'Would you like to brush your teeth now?' gives your child the chance to say either yes or no.

But by rephrasing the question:-

'When you clean your teeth, would you like to use this toothpaste or that toothpaste?' Cleaning the teeth is not an option but your child is given a choice and feels part of the decision-making.

CLEARLY STATE YOUR INTENTIONS
When... then...

'When you have washed your hands, then you can have a drink' clearly states the order in which events will happen. Ignore all protests and when it has happened, give praise to reinforce the compliance.

If... then...

This is something of a last resort, when negotiation or distraction has failed. *'If you do that, then (specific action) will happen'* is an extreme statement of intent. Praise if they comply. Do not use it if you are prepared to negotiate, or in situations that do not warrant it.

Using an 'empty threat' (one which is not carried out) sends a confusing message to the child and will make it more difficult to carry out next time, as the child will assume the *(specific action)* will not happen again.

POSITIVE AND NEGATIVE ATTENTION: THE IMPORTANCE OF PRAISE

Children need lots of praise. Whilst this may seem unnecessary or excessive to some of us, there are long-term benefits for the child. As children grow, praising helps them build a sense of positive self-esteem and confidence in their own abilities. Praise is a good form of encouragement, not just when a child achieves a goal, but also on the sometimes long and frustrating journey to a particular goal. In time, children will develop the ability to recognise when they have done well and be able to praise themselves inwardly for the achievement, with less and less need to look to others for that support. They will also be able to praise those around them, and this self-confidence will help them gain many friends as they get older.

NEGATIVE ATTENTION

The opposite of praise is criticism. Children who get criticism and negative comments for their achievements rather than praise can develop low self-esteem and become insecure. They lack confidence in their own abilities and find it more difficult to make friends; and they often seek love and praise in seemingly unloving ways.

Children crave love and attention, but when they are very young they may not be able to recognise the quality of the attention – praise and criticism both involve the parent being attentive to them. A child who is ignored when quiet and gets attention only when he or she does something that is disapproved of soon comes to learn that the way to secure a parent's time is to do something they notice, i.e. behave unacceptably. These actions reinforce parents' negative attention. In extreme cases, the child may also come to believe that being shouted at is the best form of love and attention he or she can hope for, and that this is a normal way to express the emotion. Children may also feel guilty, believing that in some way it is their fault their parents shout and seem to not like them; their parents are happy talking to others, but angry when they talk to them.

Children who are not used to being praised may appear to ignore, get embarrassed, or dismiss a positive comment when it is given to them, but they are not being 'rude' or ungrateful. They simply have not been given the opportunity to learn how to interpret and respond to what they are being told. This makes praising, positive attention and encouragement even more important for these children, and requires patience in the face of rejection. It can take time for them to learn to accept it.

POSITIVE ATTENTION

Praise is praise. It is unconditional and should never be measured. It is given for a specific achievement, or to acknowledge the effort put in to working towards the achievement, whether socially or academically.

TYPES OF PRAISE

We can praise verbally – out loud, in a passing whisper, or with the following:

- eye contact
- winking
- pat on shoulder
- clapping
- hug
- smiling
- nodding
- stroke on the head
- thumbs up

Praise – with no 'buts...'

Jack has been painting and has moved on to play with his bricks, leaving the paints out.
'That brick tower is great, Jack, but you haven't put the paints away.'

By adding *'but...'* to the praise given to Jack, the achievement of building a tower has been lost in the negative statement of not putting the paints away. Jack is more likely to remember the negative *'but you haven't...'* and forget the praise.

Better to make two statements, a praise followed by an instruction. *'That brick tower is great, Jack. Well done. (Pause to smile/reinforce.) Now put the paints away, please.'*

Other verbal praising might be:
'Wow, Hannah, you did that puzzle all by yourself.' or *'Tom, that drawing's brilliant. Well done.'*

Encouraging self-praise and praise for others

'Emily, you must feel really proud of yourself for colouring that picture in so neatly.'
'Emily, I think Sam's picture is very nice. Do you?'

Praise and conversation

Praise can be used to help children talk about their achievements and encourage them on to further goals. It also shows that you are interested in what they are doing and have understood.

Discussing a drawing:
'Susie, that's a lovely rabbit... Oh, she must be mummy... and are those her babies hiding next to the tree...? What are their names...?'

Leaving time between questions gives children a chance to answer, as they may think for some time before saying anything. Always show interest in what they say, even if it doesn't make sense.

📽 *Picture story*

PRAISING

A missed opportunity, and one that is taken

Missing an opportunity to praise may lead to the action that was requested and carried out correctly being repeated. The parent may misinterpret this as the child 'messing about' or not doing as instructed. If children have not gained the recognition in the first place they may repeat the action in the hope of gaining a response the second time.

Taking the opportunity to praise when a request is met reinforces the desire to comply the next time.

JAKE *24 months*

1 Jake's mother, Sarah, is putting the milk back in the fridge.

4 ...and it closes.

1 Sarah says 'No', reminding Jake that he is not allowed to play with the football in the house.

2 He attempts to put it down...

2 Sarah has gone to make a drink and asks Jake to close the fridge door.

3 Jake pushes the door…

5 He looks round to Sarah for a response…

6 …and then turns back towards the fridge, appearing confused.

3 …but picks it up again and decides to throw it onto the grass.

4 Sarah praises him verbally and, as Jake passes her to go into the house, she strokes his head.

BEHAVIOUR: ACCEPTABLE AND UNACCEPTABLE

Perhaps the first question should be: 'What is behaviour?'

Behave: *to act in a particular way, or to be good by acting in a way which has society's approval.*
Behaviour: *is a way of acting.*
Well behaved: *behaving in a way that is accepted as correct.*
Misbehave: *to behave badly.*

It is clear from the dictionary that *behave* and *behaviour* are quite measured words.

Once children begin to walk, they become toddlers and although on two feet and suddenly looking quite grown up, they are not. Every action a child makes can be categorised under the heading of behaviour. As adults, we classify what type of behaviour it is by applying our own standards and expectations to an action. Unfortunately for us, this has no bearing on toddlers' current perception of 'their world'. They have yet to develop an awareness or sense of danger; or to know the value of objects and why they can touch one object yet not another; or to predict the outcome of an action. A child does not understand the difference between sweets and pills, a hard or soft surface, metal or glass, or whether something is hot, cold or sharp.

Children learn through experimentation, mimicking, trial and error and repetition, so it is natural for a child who has just become mobile to want to explore everywhere – and everything. It is important for parents to check their home and do as much as possible to make it a safe place. Be particularly conscious of safety in the home: spend some time looking around at what is going to be accessible to your child and decide what you don't want to be touched. If in any doubt, pick up a leaflet at your clinic or GP's surgery. A safer home, with space for your toddler to roam and satisfy his or her natural inquisitiveness will result in less stress for everyone and prevent the need for continual nagging and repeatedly having to say *'no'*. It will also help avoid accidents and precious articles being broken.

If your toddler is into everything, and you plan to visit family or a friend's home, contact them beforehand and make them aware so that they can move things. When you arrive, have a quick look around, as each toddler may have a favourite household item they will go for; it is always better to be safe than sorry. A little time spent before you sit down can save time later and be more relaxing.

Emerging patterns of behaviour

By the time children have begun to walk, we will have a good idea of their personality and preferences. The freedom to explore and discover that comes with increased mobility is often the first time we find ourselves *'at a loss'*. Our chil-

TOM *19 months* is fascinated by cupboards. He does not understand the danger of playing in the cupboard, which is next to the oven.

dren suddenly appear to have 'minds of their own', be very determined, and never seem to listen to what we say.

If we think back to the abilities of babies at birth, what we are seeing is a rapid development made possible by being mobile. If we apply what we already know about a child in the context of age and emotional and developmental ability, it will help us respond positively and appropriately (see age-related sections later in the book).

The need for emotional support

Children who are just walking have access to far more than they can understand or process. Much of the time, this is very motivating and exciting, but equally it can become very frustrating. Not being able to mimic what they have seen adults do can result in tears, or objects being thrown. Not being able to convey what they want can trigger the same response. Equally, a great deal of what we say will have no meaning to them at all.

Unable to ask, and unable to understand, children have to learn to manage their emotions and need support from those around them. We cannot presume we know what a child is feeling as we all react differently to a situation, but we can let him or her lead us. As the child gets older and language improves, he or she will become better able to label their emotions and convey them to us.

Encouraging our children to talk can reduce frustration and help them understand their own feelings as well as those of others. In the future, this will make it easier for them to form relationships with their peers. If we can become aware of what can trigger a negative reaction, it will be much easier to plan to avoid it.

WHAT IS UNACCEPTABLE BEHAVIOUR AND WHY DOES IT HAPPEN?
The development of conflicts

What is deemed acceptable in one group may not be in another. The most obvious example is the behaviour of some football supporters. Similarly, what is acceptable in one family will not be in another, so the whole question of behaviour is subjective.

When applying standards of behaviour to our children we need to be aware of where they are developmentally, and whether or not our expectations are beyond their ability.

A great deal of children's behaviour is common within their age range, and what they display is normal for their age. Virtually every child under the age of two will say 'mine', or 'no', even when it is clear that 'no' means 'yes' (see 'Favourite words', page 156). The same applies to a great deal of what we consider to be challenging behaviour amongst preschool children. What they are displaying are normal, healthy patterns of behaviour, which, with sympathetic handling, do not persist for a long time.

Concerns by parents that their children should 'behave well' often lead them to pressure the child to behave in a way in which they are not capable (in the short term). The child's brain is not sufficiently developed to process what is being asked, and a confused response from the child may be interpreted negatively by the parent as being wilful or 'naughty'. 'Telling a child off' in these circumstances reinforces the confusion the child is feeling. As children learn by repetition, the process is likely to be repeated as they look for a consistent response. These are important learning experiences, whether a particular behaviour pattern is considered acceptable or not.

Young children are very impulsive, determined and have limited self-control, and their need to experiment and learn is almost insurmountable. Trying to prevent this can have a detrimental effect on children's confidence and self-esteem, so working patiently with children and 'steering' them, is better than being in conflict. (See 'Tantrums', page 108.)

The most positive action to help the child is to respond in a way that is acceptable by our own standards of behaviour – to teach by example.

BOUNDARIES: THE IMPORTANCE OF CONSISTENCY

Boundary: *an often imaginary line that marks the edge or limit of something.*

Establishing routines and rules, what is an acceptable standard of behaviour and what is not, and the limits we set become 'boundaries'. Children have to learn those that are flexible and those that are inflexible – boundaries for safety, such as putting a finger in a plug socket, can never be flexible. Having an extra sweet at grandma's can be. Making these boundaries clear and consistent enables children to learn which is which – flexible or not – and becomes a large part of the child's security and how they put order into their world.

The way a child learns about boundaries is by testing them, something which many of us find frustrating: '*She knows she's not supposed to do it, but she does. I'm sure she's trying to get at me*'. By repeatedly testing the boundary, a child is learning how flexible it is.

If we want our children to learn to understand our rules, then we must try to be as consistent as possible in the areas that are important to us.

Any boundaries that are set need to be attainable for the age of the child, fair, and agreed by the whole family. It is unusual for both parents to be in complete agreement, as everyone's background varies, but it is important to present the child with a united front. With more than one child, apply the same rules to both children: a rule for one and not the other is confusing and makes for a sense of insecurity and vulnerability.

Children also have to learn that different places can have different rules, and learn to modify their behaviour accordingly. It is equally important to accept some variation in the rules for special relationships: '*I don't let her do that but her grandma does*' is being critical and does not always send the clearest signal to a child who loves her grandparents.

Children are very astute and if there is disagreement between adults about the rules, in time they will be quick to play one parent off against the other. Adults can do the same, particularly in stressful situations; it can be tempting to use the child to 'get at' the other parent, which can be very damaging for the child's sense of well-being. Stress is very destructive to relationships, and we should not underestimate the levels of stress with which we live.

Children spend all their developing years challenging and checking boundaries. How they start this process has profound implications later in life.

RESPONDING TO UNACCEPTABLE BEHAVIOUR

The way we respond to unacceptable behaviour can have the opposite effect to the one we wanted to achieve. Children have very short memories and soon forget the event for which they are being punished. To respond in a severe, humiliating, leave-till-later or drawn-out way is not appropriate. '*No TV for a week*' is a meaningless gesture for a child, who is more likely to remember not being allowed to watch TV rather than why. Similarly, action taken hours after the event ('*You'll be in trouble when your father comes home*'), will not be associated with the incident, but will link the memory of a bad experience with the father, and unfairly involves him in something he was not party to. Therefore any action taken in this way is likely to make the child resentful towards the parent, rather than enabling him or her to learn from the experience.

Younger children can remember less than 30 seconds of what is being said and quite often they are unable to understand why something has happened. Lecturing, questioning, shouting, accusing or comparing one child to another doesn't help them learn about themselves or build self-esteem. In this situation it is difficult to stay calm and the tension and stress is likely to produce further conflict which can result in a child crying or the worst possible response – shutting down. The child will not be able to understand what is being said or why, and from the tone of voice, may come to believe you don't care. For a relationship to grow there has to be mutual respect and a desire to get to know each other better.

If each time we met someone they shouted at us or were aggressive, we would back off and be remote. It would not be long before we would shut them out altogether and avoid further contact. Children may feel the same, but will not able remove themselves from the situation.

Remaining calm and in control of our voice and actions is not easy in stressfull situations. It may feel as if it goes against our natural instincts, which it may do, because of our own childhood experience, but the long-term benefits to the family are enormous. However, try not to notice everything and correct it. The days can become too tense, and being too concerned with every detail can detract from the many good, positive moments that happen. Understanding the capabilities of our children as they grow can help us to be more patient and enjoy the ups and downs of parenting.

If you are able to begin with a child who is entering the toddler stage, the principles of dealing with unacceptable behaviour are easier to carry out as your child will have no other experience. The effort and hard work you put into these early days will be of benefit for life. (*See 'Changing established misbehaviour', page 60.*)

Sarah shows how, in an aggressive situation, she is able to decide when enough is enough, and walk away. Children cannot do this.

🎥 *Picture story*
LEARNING DIFFERENT RULES

From birth, babies learn by cause and effect; when they cry, their mother comes and comforts them, from which they gain reassurance.

As children explore and experiment, they continue to look to their parents for reassurance and guidance. Children will continually repeat actions to check their parents' response and by doing this they begin to learn the different rules, both flexible and inflexible.

EMILY *15 months*

Emily is learning that it is a house rule and not acceptable to put her feet on or climb on the table.

1 Emily is leaning on the table.

EMILY *15 months*

Emily is learning a more difficult rule. Sometimes she is allowed to eat food that has dropped on the floor at home but she is not allowed to eat food that has dropped on the ground outside.

1 Emily is eating raisins.

EMILY *15 months*

Emily is fascinated by 'the bin'. She is learning that she is allowed to put things in the bin, but it is not acceptable to take them out.

1 Emily touches the bin.

2 She opens it up.

3 Her mother, Corinne, immediately stops her and reminds Emily: 'No, dirty.'

2 She goes to put her leg up to climb onto the table.

3 She looks towards her mother, Corinne, for a response and her mother says, '*No.*'

4 Emily looks down at her leg as she lowers it. Corinne praises her.

2 One drops on the floor: she bends down to pick it up…

3 …and as she does, she looks up to her mother, Corinne, for her response. Corinne smiles, and Emily knows she is allowed to eat the raisin.

OPHELIA *18 months*

Ophelia has learned that it is dangerous to put her finger into the cage of the family's pet chinchilla in case she gets bitten. Very occassionally, Ophelia feels the need to see if the rule remains in place.

1 Ophelia puts her finger into the cage…

2 …and looks up to her mother, Melanie, for a response. Melanie says, '*No, dangerous.*' This confirms to Ophelia that the rule still applies.

📽 *Picture story*

STARTING TO UNDERSTAND THE RULES

Borrowing

Children show us they are beginning to understand rules and boundaries by the way they react following an incident; for example, smiling up at a parent after spilling a drink, or running away to hide. They know they have done something they should not, but have yet to learn fully what is right or what is wrong.

OPHELIA *18 months*

Whenever Ophelia sees a bag she will look in and will sometimes remove things. Ophelia's mother, Melanie, knows it will take time and patience for Ophelia to learn that the contents of a bag do not belong to her.

A friend of Melanie has come round to visit.

(See 'Favourite words', page 156.)

4 ...leaving it... and, smiling, makes steps towards her mother.

5 A little later, and with extra support from her comforter, Ophelia returns to the bag. Even though it is heavy...

6 ...she picks it up and carries it...

7 ...into the kitchen where she puts it down.

8 Ophelia is undecided what to do.

9 She ignores the bag...

1 Ophelia has spotted her mother's friend's bag and she is touching it.

2 Ophelia looks round to check Melanie's response…

3 Melanie says, 'No, Ophelia', but Ophelia manages to take a look inside the bag before…

10 ….and hides in the kitchen under the worktop. She is showing Melanie that she knows she has done something wrong.

continues overleaf…

📽 *Picture story*

STARTING TO UNDERSTAND THE RULES

continued from previous page

OPHELIA *18 months*

11 A few minutes later, Ophelia goes back to the bag and this time takes out a water bottle.

12 She rejects her comforter…

16 Melanie offers to help Ophelia by opening the bag for her.

17 Ophelia looks in the bag and spots another drink…

18 In a flash, Ophelia drops the water bottle and takes the other drink.

21 She hears Melanie coming…

22 …and throws the drink away.

23 Melanie calmy retrieves the drink and firmly tells Ophelia that it is not her drink.

13 ...to take a drink from the bottle.

14 Melanie firmly asks Ophelia to give her the bottle. She explains that it is not Ophelia's...

15 ... and she must put it back in the bag. Ophelia willingly turns towards the bag.

19 She runs with the drink into her parents' bedroom.

20 Hiding in the corner, Ophelia once again shows she knows she has done something wrong.

24 Ophelia cries out...

25 ...throws herself to the floor and kicks the wardrobe in her frustration.

26 When Ophelia has calmed and is ready to listen, Melanie explains what has happened as she gives Ophelia a drink from her own bottle.

♣ *Picture story*

DOES IT REALLY MATTER?

The actions taken by parents can change what children are expecting to happen, and they can become confused, upset or frustrated. Certain things that parents see as important are too complex for a child to understand. The question *'Does it really matter?'* needs to be considered against *'What will the upset or outcome be?'*

TOM *19 months*

Tom and his mother, Mandy, are going out.

1 Tom has picked out his coat.

4 As Mandy brings a clean sweat shirt for him, Tom tries to put the coat back on himself.

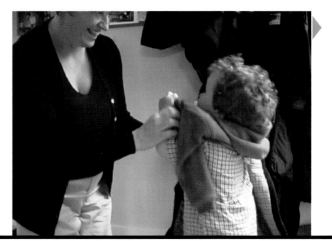

5 Mandy reassures him, but Tom's arm begins to stiffen as he realises he is not going to wear his coat.

8 He becomes calm, and once again tries to put on his coat.

9 Tom covers his head as he plays with the coat, turning it into a game.

2 After Mandy has helped Tom put on his coat, she notices some food stains down the front.

3 Mandy explains it is dirty, and she takes the coat off. For Tom, removing the coat means they are no longer going out.

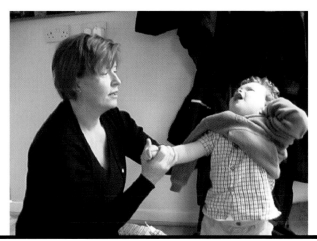

6 Tom loudly vocalises his protest and becomes unco-operative.

7 Having successfully got the sweatshirt on, Tom remains upset. Mandy gives Tom his coat.

10 Mandy distracts Tom with the house keys…

11 …and he drops the coat in his eagerness to try and unlock the door for Mandy.

IGNORING AND DISTRACTION

IGNORING

Much is said about how we shouldn't ignore our children, but there are times when it is the appropriate thing to do. To ignore a child who is doing something you disagree with or want to stop, sounds like the opposite of what you ought to be doing, but it is a powerful way of defusing potential conflict. By ignoring the child's actions, they have not achieved the result they expected – your attention. This method is very effective when used for more serious unacceptable behaviour.

To ignore means ignore. A serious face and turning the body away with no under-the-breath comments leaves the child in no doubt that his or her action has landed on stony ground. Everyone hates being ignored, and at first, the child will try even harder to gain your attention and may well use more extreme behaviour, in which case you can walk off, but consistency and perseverance will work.

Having interrupted the incident in a way that was unexpected by the child, we can now move quickly on to look for something positive that can be praised and encouraged, giving the opportunity for success. Children take time to learn and understand adult routines and rules, so for everyday little annoyances such as wingeing, sulking etc, a serious face or avoiding eye contact can be sufficient to make your view of the situation clear.

DISTRACTION

Parenting is similar to being an entertainer; skating on thin ice, thinking one step ahead whilst keeping everything on an even keel, being on the go all the time, ducking and diving – by the end of the day, your head is spinning and you're totally exhausted!

Being prepared to change what is happening at a moment's notice takes a lot of forethought, but the art of distraction is a good way to diffuse a situation before it becomes a conflict, and by being aware, you can distract the child and prevent misbehaviours or tears occurring in the first place. Quick thinking, such as simply pointing out a cat on a fence, taking a different route to avoid the sweet shop or a friend's house, may be all it takes. A small toy or a surprise ('*Let's go to the park*') can be kept as a backup. When it's wet, children get bored being cooped up indoors and tension can build. Introducing a 'rainy day box' with different toys, puzzles, etc can be useful to have as a standby. The more distraction is practised, the more enjoyable you will find your time with your child.

IGNORING
JAKE *24 months*

Jake's mother, Sarah, uses ignoring as a response to Jake's refusal to comply with an instruction. Following this sequence, she immediately uses distraction to create a positive outcome. (See 'Sarah's story', page 80.)

1 Jake screams to attract Sarah's attention, who responds by lowering her gaze.

2 Sarah continues to avoid eye contact, and Jake quietens, waiting for a response.

3 Sarah emphasises her disapproval by looking away, as Jake becomes aware his action has not succeeded.

■■ *Picture story*

DISTRACTION

TOM *19 months*

Although the radiator is not on at the moment, Tom's mother Mandy uses distraction to guide him away from the potential danger of touching a radiator, without alarming him.

1 Tom puts his hand on the radiator and looks to Mandy for her response. Mandy uses a serious face and says, 'No.'

2 Tom chooses to ignore her and places his hand into the gap in the radiator…

3 …pretending his hand has become stuck, and looks around, laughing. Mandy repeats, 'No.'

4 Mandy ignores Tom's attempt to start a game, and distracts him by offering him a ball to put away. Tom spots a yellow ball under the radiator.

5 He happily takes the balls and runs to put them away. Mandy joins in and praises him.

CHANGING ESTABLISHED MISBEHAVIOUR

There are no quick fixes – but it is worth it in the end

Children continually test boundaries and they quickly learn how to exploit any inconsistencies between parents to their own advantage. They have also learned that certain behaviours are acceptable, some are not, and some are negotiable. It is the negotiable actions that are the most difficult to modify, because from experience, children know that if they are persistent enough, their parents may just relent.

Making changes to improve behaviour is not easy, and it should involve every member of the family, not just be the responsibility of the child. It takes time, and parents should be mindful of this. They need to be consistent, and show great patience whilst they support, encourage and praise all attempts by children to modify their behaviour.

📽 *Picture story*

RHIANNA *4 years*

Rhianna's mother, Natalia, has always kept the sweets in the top kitchen cupboard... 'a safe place and out of the way'. Rhianna soon learned where they were kept, and often climbs up to get herself a treat. Natalia and Rhianna's father, Paul, have tried various methods to stop her, without success. From today, Natalia is going to show her disapproval by using a stern neutral face, and no discussion. She will then distract Rhianna by involving her in the decision to move the location of the 'treats'.

4 As Rhianna climbs, she seems unaware of the potential dangers all around her. She is also wearing socks and could easily slip.

5 Rhianna has to stand on the kitchen work surface to enable her to reach the cupboard.

6 She hears Natalia coming and, having taken something, starts to shut the cupboard door.

10 Natalia explains to Rhianna that she may have sweets from the cupboard only when she has asked, and the answer has been 'Yes.'

11 Natalia involves Rhianna by asking her to decide what they should use to put the treats in. Rhianna chooses to use a pink bowl.

12 Natalia squats down and together they put the treats into the new bowl.

1 Rhianna walks into the kitchen.

2 In an attempt to stop Rhianna climbing, Natalia and Paul removed the handles from the drawers.

3 Rhianna has found a way round the problem. She opens the bottom draw and uses it as a step.

7 Rhianna has taken a packet of sweets but she makes no attempt to hide them. She is still learning about deception and Rhianna shows she is honest and unable to lie. (*See 'Truthfulness', page 286.*)

8 Natalia calmly takes the sweets from Rhianna and with a serious face, says: '*No.*'

9 She lifts Rhianna down from the worktop, and reminds her of the dangers. Natalia now tells her that the treats are going to be moved to a lower cupboard.

13 Natalia makes space in the new cupboard for the bowl. She explains again about not climbing, and that Rhianna should ask before she takes a treat.

14 Some time later, Rhianna asks her mother if she can have a treat.

15 This time, Natalia agrees, and lets Rhianna select a treat from the new cupboard.

📽 *Picture story*

WHEN MISBEHAVIOURS RETURN

Rhianna is given a consistent message

Rhianna has climbed up to take treats from the cupboard for a long time. On previous occasions, her mother, Natalia, or her father, Paul, would come and lift her down. Sometimes they would be cross with her and not let her have a treat, and other times they would smile and give her a treat. The inconsistency reinforces Rhianna's belief that if she climbs, she may get a treat. Because of this, and despite the fact that she knows the cupboard with the treats has changed, Rhianna will still climb up on occasions to try and see if there is anything in the old cupboard.

By being calm, and consistently responding in the same way, Rhianna is now receiving a clear signal from her mother and her father that climbing is unacceptable and does not result in a treat.

RHIANNA *4 years*

1 Rhianna and Natalia are in the kitchen.

4 Natalia approaches Rhianna, and with a serious face, calmly but firmly says, 'No.'

SMALL STEPS LEAD TO BIGGER STEPS

During the weeks that follow, Natalia and Paul praise Rhianna whenever they notice her do anything, however small, that is a positive step towards her new routine.

The rewarding times. Rhianna's mother, Natalia, praises her at every opportunity, reinforcing her positive behaviour, and her sense of self-esteem.

2 While Natalia is occupied at the sink, Rhianna climbs up onto the work surface.

3 When Natalia turns around, she sees Rhianna on the work surface.

5 Without further words, and keeping her face serious, Natalia lifts Rhianna from the worktop...

6 ...puts her down on the floor and leaves the kitchen – Rhianna is motionless: this is not the response she expected.

1 Rhianna is standing on the drawer. Sometimes she still wants to see what is in the old cupboard.

2 This time Rhianna decides not to climb up, and as she drops her foot to the ground...

3 ...Natalia, who saw this, immediately praises her action, rewarding Rhianna with a hug.

SECTION TWO

SARAH'S STORY

BEFORE... THE BEGINNING OF A PARTNERSHIP

HELEN AND CLIVE SAY...

'We first worked with Sarah whilst producing *The Social Baby*, when Jake was only one week old. Two years later, whilst recruiting families for *The Social Toddler*, we happened to meet Sarah and Jake again at a schools swimming event. Jake was running around and Sarah was obviously finding him a handful. This prompted us to approach her and see if she would like to take part in this book. Sarah was very keen and immediately volunteered to be filmed; she also seemed pleased that we might be able to help her with Jake.

When we were ready to film, Helen phoned Sarah to find out a little more about Jake: what he was like and if there were any changes she would like to see happen. Sarah sighed, saying she couldn't take him shopping because he was a nightmare; he'd go mad when Mark came home from work; he likes putting on her make-up (which she found a bit worrying) and he's just always being 'naughty'.

We explained to Sarah that we would video as if we weren't there, and for her to carry on as if it was a normal morning with Jake. After the session, we said we would study the video, and then return to work with her and Jake.'

SARAH SAYS...

'Ever since my son, Jake, has been able to walk, life has been a headache. I think overnight it was a big change for Mark and I, and especially Jake too. I thought he was touching things I didn't want him to on purpose to irritate me, because he could see he was getting my attention. All I seemed to be doing was telling him off all the time.

Jake has always been a handful. I thought I was a bad mother for the way he behaved whilst out shopping, visiting family and just generally everyday. He would run around the supermarket like it was an assault course. He would throw his lunch at me or on the floor, and would not eat it. He would throw his toys at me, and it goes on... It got to the point where I put him in a private nursery one morning a week just so I could go shopping peacefully! I was getting very irritable with him and was finding myself shouting at him all the time. I felt like there was never a good time with him...

When Clive and Helen first approached me to take part in their second book, I was very honoured and excited. I also thought all I would be doing was posing for a few pictures with Jake! Little did I know these fantastic people were going to change Mark and my life with Jake dramatically!'

📽 *Picture story*

DRAWING

The first video session lasted for two hours. Jake had played with his train set, and it has been cleared away. Sarah now gets the chalk board out for Jake to have a drawing activity.

1 Jake is keen to start drawing. He has picked up a piece of chalk and put it in his mouth.

2 He looks to Sarah for her response. S: *'Don't put the chalk in your mouth.'*

6 Jake hides under the easel. Sarah picks the chalk up...

7 ...and gives it back to him. Jake drops another. S: *'Oh dear.'*

8 He looks to Sarah for her response.

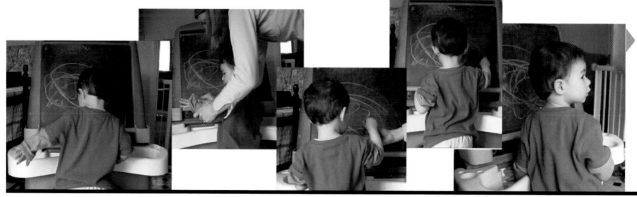

12 Sarah leaves his side. Jake uses his hand to rattle the chalks about in the tray. S: *'Don't do that.'*

13 *'Don't 'cos you'll get dirty and I'll put it away. Do it properly.'* Sarah rolls his sleeves up. She then gives him a chalk. *'Use pink.'*

14 Jake uses the pink chalk and looks around for Sarah's response. There is not one, and Jake rattles the chalk again.

3 Jake puts the chalk behind his back, and then throws it onto the floor.

4 S: *'Pick it up.'* Jake makes no attempt to.

5 Sarah takes a biscuit away from him, which he has been eating. S: *'Pick it up.'*

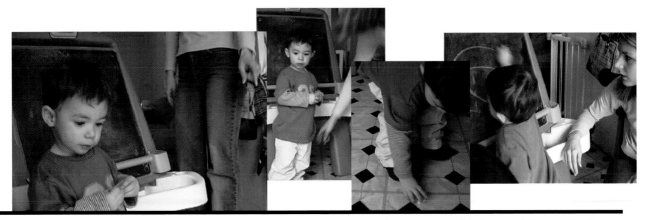

9 S: *'Let's go and pick it up....'*

10 *'...Mummy pick one up, and you pick one up. Good boy.'*

11 Jake draws, whilst Sarah talks about the different coloured chalk.

15 Jake then throws a piece of chalk. He waits for Sarah's response.

16 S: *'Pick it up.'*

17 Jake picks up the chalk.

continues overleaf...

📽 *Picture story*

FROM DRAWING TO FRIDGE MAGNETS ...does it really matter?

continued from previous page

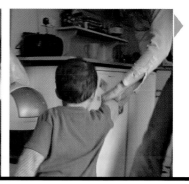

18 Jake finds a fridge magnet amongst the chalks. He tries to put the magnet on the chalk board, but finds it does not stay. S: '*Put it on the fridge.*' Jake does not repond.

19 S: '*Come on...*'

20 '*...Put it...*'

24 S: '*Put it back on the fridge. Come on.*' J: '*No.*' Jake throws it on the floor. S: '*Right, it's going away.*'

25 Jake then grabs some chalks from the tray...

26 ...and then runs off into the living room.

COPYING A HOUSEHOLD ACTIVITY

1 Jake sweeps, as Sarah holds the dustpan. She then gets a drink.

2 Jake continues sweeping. He momentarily stops to listen to a plane. S: '*Mummy finish it.*' J. '*No.*'

3 After sweeping up well, Jake looks round for Sarah's response.

21 '...On here.'

22 Jake takes two fridge magnets and looks at the backs of them. He walks towards the chalk board.

23 S: 'No, they go on the fridge.' Jake drops one. He looks to Sarah.

27 Sarah brings him back.

28 S: 'Put that back on the fridge.'

29 Jake puts the fridge magnet back on the fridge. He looks to Sarah for her response.

4 He puts together the brush and pan.

5 S 'That's it, mummy finish. Come on, let mummy do it now. All done.'

▣ *Picture story*

LUNCH TIME

Sarah has made Jake a sandwich for lunch.

1 Sarah has sat Jake at the table and gives him a sandwich.

2 Jake has tried to take his bib off. S: *'Leave it on. Don't play with it.'* (Referring to the food.)

3 Sarah sits at the table to drink her tea. *'Try and eat it properly, please.'*

7 Jake points to the juice bottle.

8 He gets up. S *'Eat your dinner.'* As Jake plops down in his chair the cushion makes a noise. He repeats the movement three times.
S: *'D'you want me to smack your bum?'*

11 Jake pushes the plate away. Sarah pushes it back.

12 Jake throws a piece of bread, Sarah puts it back on the plate.
S: *'Eat it one at a time.'*
Jake throws the bread to Sarah, who throws it back to Jake.

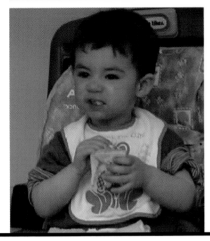

4 S: *'Do you want a Bob?* (Yoghurt pudding.) *Eat it properly.'*

5 Jake first holds up his sandwich, then juice bottle. S: *'Juice.'*

6 S: *'No. Eat your sandwich first.'* Sarah removes the bottle.

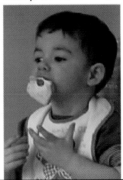

9 Sarah approaches Jake. *'Pack it in.'*

10 Jake responds. S: *'Don't throw it. Stop it. Eat it properly.'*

14 As Jake eats his pudding, he spits some out to have a look. S: *'Don't do that. Don't be disgusting. Eat it properly otherwise I'll take it away. Abi can have it.'* (Abi is the family dog.)

13 Jake resists Sarah's attempts to persuade him to eat any more.

📽 *Picture story*

A TRIP TO THE SUPERMARKET

Sarah finds shopping with Jake very difficult, especially in a supermarket.

Jake shows he finds Sarah's use of language confusing and frustrating.

Sarah and Jake arrive at the supermarket.

Jake points to the biscuits.

S: *'Get some cookies for later. Yeah?'*
S: *'Do you want Bob the Builder?'* He hits and kicks.

Jake points to some more biscuits.

Out of the trolley, Jake points to a cake. Sarah gives him one. J: *'Car.'*
S: *'Come on.'*

Back in the trolley, he calms. Sarah shows him some juice.

S: *'Jake, come back.'*

At the check-out. S: *'Will you help me?'*

J: 'Nana.' S: 'Yes, Nana.'

S: 'No. Can have one when you get home.'

Jake asks for 'nana' (a banana) on and off for six minutes.

J: 'Please.'

Jake feels restricted. He kicks out.

He puts them in the trolley.

Now walking, he wants a biscuit.

S: 'Don't touch, That's not ours.' J: 'Cat.'

J: 'Car.'

Jake comes back. Sarah doesn't respond: Jake goes again.

They leave.

AFTER THE FIRST VIDEO SESSIONS...

HELEN AND CLIVE...

'It was apparent whilst filming, that Sarah and Jake were not enjoying each other's company as much as they could be. Whatever they did seemed to turn quickly into a conflict, and once started, they found it difficult to end the cycle of events. There were happy moments and smiles, but mostly we just saw frustration, conflict and anger – in a stressed-out, tired mum and a confused little boy. We left with a sense of sadness.

When we looked at the video, what came across strongly is that we were observing a family that was *so close* to being everything it wanted to be. What seemed to trigger conflicts were not a result of Jake suffering from major conduct disorder, or from Sarah being a dreadful mother. Sarah clearly adores her son, and like all of us, wants him to grow into a lovely, well mannered, and liked child. Sarah was putting herself under a lot of pressure to try and make Jake behave in a way that she believed society expects. In turn, a great deal of her expectations for Jake were unrealistic, and her use of language and words such as *'properly'* and *'later'* were beyond the comprehension of a two-year-old.

We also noticed how well ordered Sarah's house was. It seemed that any activity for Jake was on a timer, and it would be whisked away and cleaned up almost before it had started. Sarah would remain by Jake's side, and make sure the activity was carried out in the way *she* thought it should be done: Sarah would spend much of her time asking Jake to do things in a different way, or she would interrupt and show him.

We felt Sarah would need to try to relax more around the house and expect to have some untidiness with a lively two-year-old. This would then enable her to take a step back from an activity and let Jake have the space to play and experiment, as well as have some control over his activities. This may sound simple, but for a tidy and ordered person like Sarah, it can represent a huge change in mind set – to be able to watch seeming chaos evolve, and then to leave it.

We noticed Jake was continually doing anything that would attract Sarah's attention and then looking for her response (*see 'Learning different rules', page 50*). If Jake did do something good, Sarah either did not appear to notice, or seemed relieved and said nothing. Unfortunately, Sarah responded more to Jake when he did something that she did not want him to do. In these circumstances a negative pattern of behaviour was being reinforced.

Most importantly for us, we knew Sarah was very receptive to what we were doing, and she was desperate to improve both her relationship with Jake, and his behaviour. Sarah was also keen to listen and try what we suggested, she trusted our input, and we developed a close and positive working relationship together. We emphasised that any changes would require the support of Mark and the whole family; it could be hard work, and Jake may get worse before he improved.

The following pages show our next video sessions. We began by asking Sarah to write down how she felt about Jake on two lists. First her dislikes, and then her likes (*see overleaf*). We then discussed with Sarah what we'd observed previously, and repeated some of the activites; but this time, Helen worked together with Sarah, helping and supporting her before and during the activities. The following day, Sarah took part in a parenting session (*see 'We may be adults but we can still pretend', pages 28-37*) and a few weeks later we returned to the supermarket.'

SARAH, MARK AND JAKE...

'The first time Clive and Helen came round all they did was watch and film how Jake and I interacted with each other. I kept thinking to myself 'am I doing this right? Am I dealing with him how a mother should? Or am I totally messing this up?' They filmed us for about 2 hours having lunch and playing and Jake being naughty! (That's what I thought anyway!) When I started to do this project with Clive and Helen, I didn't think Jake would be able to change his 'naughty' ways.

A couple of weeks later Clive called me to ask if they could come round and try dealing with Jake differently, which might help me not get so frustrated at him. Well, I couldn't turn down an offer like that! Everything that was filmed previously, we went over and dealt with the situation differently. It was like I got out a magic wand and his 'bad' behaviour had disappeared. I seemed to have a completely different child. But it wasn't Jake that had changed, it was ME!!!!

When Clive and Helen asked me to participate in a role-play parenting session with them, I started to put myself in Jake's shoes (see 'We may be adults but we can still pretend', pages 28-37). The role-play was between myself, Helen and another lady. I was asked to kneel down whilst Helen stood on a table (to show the height differece between an adult and child). I was then asked to try and get Helen's attention but without talking, as most two-year-olds can't talk. I did this, but Helen kept ignoring me and I was getting very frustrated and angry (Sarah was playing a child, Helen an adult). She also talked very badly about me with another 'parent' which made me feel very upset. Another role-play that we did was Helen telling me off, shouting at me as she was towering over me, and this was quite scary!! Throughout the whole session, all I kept thinking of was how badly I had treated my son.

After the session I found myself stepping back for a moment and thinking why was Jake doing what he was doing and how I had not taken his needs into consideration or how he might be feeling. I feel this influenced me to change the way I was dealing with Jake. To my advantage, the relationship between my son and I is much better and we communicate very well now. I am very aware now of how I deal with Jake. I never call him names or put him down; I am always praising him for good things he does and helping him when he needs it.'

📽 *Picture story*

A NEW START

Having studied the video footage, we noticed some key areas where we felt Sarah might benefit if she was made aware: her use of language, giving Jake some personal space, ignoring negatives and praising positives.

When we next visited Sarah and Jake a couple of weeks later, Sarah had not had a good night with Jake. He had developed a rash and kept waking; they were both tired. We asked if they would prefer us to come back another day, but Sarah said she had so been looking forward to the day she was sure it would be fine.

First, we asked Sarah to write down what she does not like about Jake. We then asked her to write down what she does like about him.

1 Sarah writes down her views. She says she found it easy to write down Jake's bad points but found it more difficult to write about his good points. She had never really thought about her feelings towards him in that way.

5 Next, Helen asks Sarah if Jake's clothes can get wet. Sarah says, *'Yes, but I'd roll his sleeves up.'*

6 Sarah tightens the hot tap and explains to Jake that the cold tap is the one for him to use and says, *'Jake's tap.'*

7 Jake begins the washing up activity.

11 Jake plays happily as he pours water from one container to another. Helen tells Sarah how much Jake is learning from this kind of play.

12 Jake has turned the cold tap on too much and it sprays out. Sarah shows him how to turn it down. He assists her and she praises his efforts.

13 Sarah notices the chair is in danger of slipping and she wedges it safely in place. Helen suggests this type of observation can become part of Sarah's forward planning.

Sarah reflects: *'The questionnaire made me realise that there are so many more things that I enjoy about Jake. And all the bad things are irrelevant.'*

2 Helen and Sarah sit together on the sofa. Helen tells Sarah that she is putting Sarah's negative thoughts about Jake aside. Now they are going to look at, and build on, Sarah's positive comments about Jake.

3 Sarah said earlier that Jake likes a new activity – washing up. Helen suggests Jake might like to do this now. Sarah is keen to begin. Helen slows her down, and asks if she prepares the area for Jake first.

4 Sarah says she only removes sharp objects from the sink. Helen makes Sarah aware of surrounding objects, the work-surface area, floor and the chair that Jake will use. Is it OK if they are all used or get wet?

8 Helen suggests that Sarah sits down and chats while Jake plays. Sarah says, *'I would never have thought of sitting down and letting him get on with it. Normally I let him do a few things and then finish it off myself.'*

9 Helen points out that Sarah has prepared the area and that she can keep an eye on him from the table. Helen also encourages Sarah to praise Jake at every opportunity.

10 Jake has spilled some water down his T-shirt. He has come to Sarah to be wiped. Helen makes Sarah aware of an opportunity for closer contact between them: to kiss, and say, *'Well done.'*

14 Jake looks round as he is cleaning his bottle and water spills onto the floor.

15 Jake is shown that if he tips the bottle upside down he needs to do it over the sink so that the water remains in the sink.

16 Next time he is successful and Sarah praises him.
(Jake happily played 'washing up' for three-quarters of an hour.)

📽 *Picture story*

DRAWING

The next activity for Jake is to do some drawing. Sarah feels she should change Jake's clothes. Helen suggests that Sarah asks herself: *'Do I want a clean top that might get dirty with chalk dust, or shall I leave Jake in his vest so that it doesn't matter if it gets dirty? I can always change him later.'* Jake is keen to begin, so Sarah opts for the latter.

1 Preparation is made…

2 …and Jake begins to draw on the chalk board.

6 Jake switches to the paper and Helen encourages Sarah to praise him. She does: *'Good boy.'*

7 Jake happily continues to draw on the paper, now using different coloured chalks.

8 Sarah gets down to talk to Jake about the different coloured chalks. She is surprised when Jake says that all the chalks are coloured blue. (*See 'Categorising', page 148.*)

12 Jake puts his picture on the fridge, and, once more, looks to Sarah for her response. Sarah shows her approval.

13 In Jake's efforts to use the fridge magnets to hold his picture up, one drops on the floor. He retrieves it and again, Sarah praises him.

14 Jake decides to play with the fridge magnet.

3 Sarah sits down and gives Jake some space by watching him from a distance. She admires his drawing.

4 Helen suggests letting Jake try using different media – paper, pens and crayons. Sarah finds some for him.

5 Jake tries to use the pen on the chalkboard. Sarah immediately says, *'No, Jake, do it on the paper.'*

9 He drops the red chalk. We ask: *'Where's the chalk gone? Can anyone see it?'* Jake looks, and he picks it up. S: *'Clever boy.'*

10 Jake is pleased with his drawing and trumphantly turns round for Sarah's response.

11 Sarah praises his efforts and claps. She says: *'That's lovely. Do you want to put it on the fridge for Daddy?'*

15 He has removed the picture and shows Sarah again. She praises it again, this time saying how clever he is.

16 Sarah bends down and tries to kiss Jake, but he is far too excited…

17 …and runs off, shouting in his delight.

🎥 *Picture story*

LUNCH TIME

Time to chat together

We noticed previously that Sarah tidies up and puts things away immediately after each activity, which doesn't give Jake a chance to go back to it. Sarah says she does this because she likes the house tidy. Helen suggests that on this occasion, an advantage in leaving the activities out is that Sarah can get on with making lunch while Jake happily plays at the sink.

1 Sarah prepares lunch while Jake 'washes up'. Helen suggests Sarah can still keep an eye on him and continue to praise his efforts.

2 Sarah turns and looks at Jake. She remarks that she has never praised him so much in one hour as she has today. She comments that before, she always just picked out what Jake was doing wrong. Her new approach makes sense: *'Everyone likes to be praised.'*

6 Sarah engages Jake in conversation.

7 She lets Jake know how good he has been today.

8 Sarah listens to Jake asking about what is in their sandwiches. She shows Jake she has the same in hers.

12 Next, Jake puts his comforter in his drink. Sarah disapproves and says: *'Please don't, Jake.'*

13 Helen advises Sarah that if this is deemed unacceptable, she should not negotiate but act immediately: remove the comforter from Jake...

14 ...and put it away, out of sight. There will be no discussion.

3 While Sarah prepares the sandwiches, Helen suggests she might cut Jake's a little smaller. She noticed he was having trouble handling them before, and this may make it easier.

4 Sarah pushes Jake's chair in, ready for him to eat lunch. Helen invites Sarah to join him so that they can eat lunch together. Sarah says she would normally not do this, but would eat as she tidies around the kitchen.

5 Although Sarah sits at the table with Jake, she does not talk to him. Helen suggests this is an ideal time to chat together about the events of the morning.

9 Jake eats his sandwich in his own time and in his own way. This time, Sarah feels no need to comment about how he is eating.

10 Jake pushes his plate away, showing he has finished.

11 Sarah feels Jake has not eaten enough. She says she normally offers him a yoghurt or crisps, and asks what she should do now. Helen replies that he has made his own decision, and that he will eat more later, when he is hungry.

15 Jake screams. Sarah ignores him, averts her eyes and remains serious-faced. Jake does not expect this response and continues to scream.

16 Sarah looks away from Jake. He looks surprised and quickly quietens.

17 Sarah distracts Jake by drawing his attention to some colourful patterns on the placemat, and a conversation continues.

▣ *Picture story*

RETURN TO THE SUPERMARKET

This time, a shared activity

Before we leave the house for the supermarket, Helen suggests that Sarah might like to pack a small bag of 'goodies' to bring with her, in case Jake gets bored or hungry. Sarah packs two toys, a drink and some fruit. Sarah has written a shopping list which she shows Helen, who suggests that any items for Jake are selected last. This may help reduce his frustration.

1 Helen asks Sarah to give Jake a choice: does he want to go in the trolley or not? He chooses not to, and Sarah states his boundaries: if he runs off, he will be put in the trolley. Jake appears to listen and understand.

2 Helen encourages Sarah to let Jake become involved in the shopping. She directs him to the lettuces.

6 Sarah gives Jake the list to hold.

7 He goes back and gets another lettuce. Sarah says, *'Just one...'*

8 *'...Put it back.'*

12 Jake initially gets a wrong (large) milk carton, but Sarah helps him to succeed, and he carries the correct carton to the trolley. S: *'Clever boy.'*

13 Sarah lifts up Jake so that he can pick out a loaf of bread.

14 He wants to be put down so that he can place the loaf into the trolley by himself.

3 Jake surveys the lettuces…

4 …and chooses one. S: *'That one…*

5 …*into the trolley.'* Jake puts the lettuce in the trolley. S: *'Good boy.'*

9 Jake very carefully puts back the lettuce, and Sarah praises him: *'Good boy.'*

10 She then encourages him to come with her: *'This way, Jake.'*

11 Sarah points to some milk and asks Jake to get one carton.

15 Next, they go down the sweet aisle. Sarah plans ahead and lets Jake push the trolley. He is so focussed that he does not seem to notice all the possible treats that are on display all around him.

continues overleaf…

📽 *Picture story*

RETURN TO THE SUPERMARKET *continued from previous page*

16 Towards the end of the aisle, Jake's favourite cartoon character catches his eye.

17 Sarah brings out his toy and says, *'Show train round the supermarket.'* For a sufficiently brief moment, his attention is diverted.

18 However, Jake returns quickly, wanting to help. Sarah moves to get a juice bottle down. Jake protests.

22 Sarah stays calm and thinks quickly as she moves the bread out of the way to the the front part of the trolley. Jake drops in the juice bottle.

23 Sarah gives Jake a drink as they move on.

24 Jake decides to sit on the cat litter with his drink. Sarah puts some other items in the trolley. While he is sat happily drinking, Helen suggests to Sarah she may like to interest Jake in the things around him. Shopping is a good activity for learning.

28 He picks one out and kisses it. He puts it in the trolley and Sarah praises him.

29 Jake pushes the trolley towards the check-out.

30 At the checkout, Helen suggests Jake may like to put the items from the trolley onto the counter. While they wait, Helen encourages Sarah to involve Jake and look at the next shopper's items.

19 Sarah lifts him up, *'You get it.'* Jake drags the bottle from the shelf.

20 S: *'Shall I?'* J:. *'No. Don't.'*

21 Sarah takes the bottle of juice from Jake and almost puts it in the trolley. Jake squeals his protest, his fists clenched and arms raised.

25 Sarah starts: *'Where's the cat's nose?'* He points, and a brief game of identification starts.

26 Sarah's final item is Jake's favourite yoghurt. She has remembered to get it last and although it is at the wrong end of the shop, Jake enthusiastically runs ahead of the trolley to find it.

27 Jake shouts, *'Bob'*, as he points the yoghurt out to Sarah.

31 Helen suggests Jake may like to sit and help pack. The assistant reminds Jake to be mindful of his fingers on the conveyor belt. Jake eagerly collects the shopping and puts it in the bags.

32 Jake has taken the receipt from the assistant. Sarah gives him some change. From start to finish, Sarah and Jake have together shared in the shopping.

MARK...

'When Sarah told me she was going to be in an 'experiment' with Jake, I didn't really take much notice to be honest. Like Sarah says, Jake has always been a handful. I haven't really got to see much of this as I am at work all day. But I could always tell if Sarah'd had a bad day by the way she was when I got home from work. Most of the time she was moody and tired and was in bed by 8pm. So I didn't really have much time with her.

After Clive and Helen had given her advice about Jake, things started to get better. Jake seemed to be a delight to be around with, instead of being a little devil. And Sarah seemed to be chilling out a lot more. She started to give me a kiss when I got home and we started talking about the day she'd had with Jake. But the difference was, she was excited to be telling me what she and Jake had done that day. The biggest difference is that I'm not afraid to go home at the end of the day!!!!!'

SARAH...

'Seeing the change in both myself and Jake encouraged me to carry on with this method of raising Jake. I feel that myself, Mark and Jake have learned more about each other and we now have patience, understanding and more respect for one another.

I know this sounds very clichéd, but this did not happen overnight, this took time and a lot of hard work and communication between the three

of us, but it has paid off! The only advice I would give to someone is, once you start, stick it out, because the reward is fantastic!!

The things that I never let him do before, like washing up, I found myself letting him do it! I was finding more things around the house for him to do which I normally wouldn't have. Simple things like this made my life so much more peaceful! Even Mark, has noticed the difference, as the atmosphere he comes home to now is more tranquil!

My family has been very understanding but they think that I have changed more than Jake, which is probably true! They can't believe how much patience I have with him now. Sometimes they say *'Oh Sarah, just smack him, he's being naughty.'* But he isn't, he is just trying to communicate with me in a different way from how other children would.

Whereas I couldn't take Jake supermarket shopping, I take him there now as a day trip. He loves it! I have since bought him his own trolley and he goes around with a pretend list, throwing stuff in his trolley. So what if I don't need it? I can leave it at the check-out. I enjoy seeing him enjoying himself and for me that is one of the greatest gifts I am able to give him!!!

We feel we are now more of a family.'

HILTON DAVIS... *Child Health Psychologist*

'This is a wonderful story, not only because those involved (Jake, Sarah, Mark, Helen and Clive) gained a great deal, but because it illustrates many important aspects of the helping process.

Communication is never simple, and this story demonstrates the ease with which good people can become mismatched in understanding, develop a negative cycle of interaction, and have their confidence and well-being eroded. It clearly portrays the natural difficulties for parents of adapting to the complex situation of understanding children, whose skills are limited, whose world view is so different and whose needs are so rapidly changing.

It illustrates the importance and nature of the relationship with potential helpers. Sarah knew she needed help with Jake, as we all do at times, and had the courage to open up such an intimate aspect of her life to Helen and Clive. They honoured this privilege by working in partnership with her. Respecting and using her expertise, they worked alongside her in ways that not only helped resolve the problems, but also restored her faith in herself, even while challenging her to think and act differently.

It illustrates the need for careful exploration and understanding of problems and how better to do this than with film and discussion?

This story clearly portrays the main message of the book, that of respecting children as individual, thinking people, and the need for empathy. With help, Sarah not only managed to be open to Jake and to try to understand his picture of the world, she had the humility and strength to change and the generosity of spirit to give what Jake needed. However, she also demonstrated an important principle that making every effort to fit in with children's needs pays huge dividends in them fitting in with you.'

SECTION THREE

THE SECOND YEAR

PHYSICAL AND EMOTIONAL DEVELOPMENT

▶ *Picture story*
MOBILITY (1)

The age at which children become able to walk can vary
enormously. Some may walk by themselves at 9 months,
but others may not take their first steps until towards the end of
their second year. Continual practice helps refine the control
and use of muscles, so that they become more competent at
walking and changing position.

MEGAN *12 months*

1 Megan's mother, Kelly, holds her
steady. Megan vocalises her
excitement and reaches out her hands
towards a friend.

2 Megan makes great efforts to lift
her leg and take a step forward.

3 She turns to Kelly and together they
share Megan's success.

SAPPHIRE *14 months*

1 Sapphire relies on her mother, Zoë,
to help her to walk around the
garden.

2 Sapphire makes great efforts to
transfer her weight from one foot...

3 ...to the other.

EMILY *15 months*

Although Emily can walk quite efficiently, she finds changing position from sitting to squatting takes great effort.

1 Emily has just bumped to the floor, her legs out in front of her.

2 She transfers her weight forward, placing her hands on the floor…

3 …and using her thigh muscles, pushes up her bottom, enabling her right leg to drag backwards.

4 Emily finds that her right foot is being prevented from moving by her left foot.

5 She now makes a huge considered effort to free the foot and swing it out to the side.

6 Balanced, she can now bring her feet closer together.

7 By pushing her bottom down, she transfers her weight backwards …

8 …and by bringing her head and arms up…

9 …Emily is in the squat position and can resume her play.

MOBILITY (2)

Mastering the skills of balance and co-ordination needed to get up, walk, run, climb and negotiate objects takes a great deal of repetition and practice. Children also have to learn about different gradients and uneven surfaces, being barefoot or wearing different footwear.

The single-minded determination to succeed in this area is overwhelming and exhausting, so it is not surprising that children keep going until they flop to the ground and look to an adult to carry them.

📽 *Picture story*
MEGAN *12 months*

Being fearless, Megan takes any opportunity to practise climbing the stairs. She is not yet able to stand on her own and her mother, Kelly, distracts her away from a potentially dangerous situation.

4 Kelly distracts Megan by standing her on the floor. She throws her arms and hands out as she tries to balance.

TOM *19 months*

Being competent at walking, Tom is now able to experiment with movement. He confidently links together several complex movements and clearly gets great pleasure from his achievement!

1 Tom shuffles along the floor on his knees – making use of the slippery surface.

1 Megan lifts her left leg onto the first step.

2 As she gets her right foot on the step, she stands up and turns, shakily, to Kelly, who comes towards her.

3 Kelly explains to Megan that she could fall, and lifts her from the stairs. Megan vocalises her protest.

5 She uses all her concentration and determination, but twists and wobbles.

6 Although she regains her balance…

7 …Megan drops to the floor, reverting to her more practised crawl to get her about.

2 He spins round to a sitting position…

3 …before rolling over and round.

📽 *Picture story*

CLIMBING

Fearlessness

Children love to climb. It is an exciting challenge that enables them to see the world from a different perspective. However, they are also fearless and the need to climb makes them unaware of possible dangers they may encounter.

Being attentive and alert to potential danger, removing temptations and offering repeated guidance can help prevent serious injury.

MONA *16 months*
Mona slowly climbs up to stand on her push-along car.

EMILY *17 months*
Emily has just started to climb up on furniture.

1 Emily has climbed onto the garden bench and is stamping her feet.

2 She steps nears to the edge of the bench and peers to the ground...

EMIL *20 months*   *Emil can now confidently climb up on the window seat.*

1 Emil has no need to look where he places his feet...

2 ...as he climbs onto the window seat.

3 Emil's co-ordination enables him to run confidently along the seat.

1 Mona watches where she places her left foot as she steps onto her car.

2 With her foot firmly on the car, Mona gingerly straightens her knees and, using her hands to balance herself,…

3 …Mona stands up straight and releases her hands. She is greeted with a big smile from her mother, Nadira.

3 …her mother, Corinne, alerts Emily to the possible danger and lifts her off.

4 Corinne invites Emily to 'tap dance' on a safe metal drain cover.

4 However, as he takes a leap onto his push-along horse…

5 …he misjudges the height that his leg needs to clear the back of the horse…

6 …causing the horse and himself to fall over.

FINE MOTOR SKILLS

Dexterity

Even before birth hands and fingers are used for exploration. From an early age children use the whole of either hand, in what is known as a palmer grasp, to hold an object. During the second year children continue to do this, when holding a brush or similar, to make marks on paper. But they also refine their ability to pick up small objects by using a pincer grasp: bringing together the tips of the index finger and thumb. This refined ability enables us to skilfully use our hands; to make and use tools.

Children can now point to things of interest using the index finger, and pick up and investigate objects by rotating the wrist and turning them over.

📽 *Picture story* ▶

EMILY *15 months*

Emily has picked up a cotton reel from the toy basket and is looking at it intently.

EMILY *15 months* uses the pincer grasp to pick up a raisin. She mimics the grasping movements with her left hand.

JADE *16 months* and EMIL *20 months* are using the palmer grasp.

1 Emily has grasped the cotton reel and is holding it firmly with her two hands, which enables her to have a good look.

2 Emily rotates her wrists and has poked her right finger into one end of the cotton reel. She then turns her wrist. She can now put her left finger into the other hole.

3 Her concentration is broken and the cotton reel slips off her fingers. As her dexterity skills improve, she will be able to explore more about the world around her.

EMILY *15 months* uses her index finger to point to something of interest.

MICHA *12 months* and LAURANCE *13 months* are using their hands to explore in the sensory room.

MONA *16 months* is now almost able to drink from a cup by herself.

CHANGES IN SLEEP PATTERNS

Emotional development and physical achievement are closely linked and, as children progress, previously established routines for sleep can be upset; a sleep pattern of two daytime naps becomes less frequent and one sleep in the afternoon more the norm. If this sleep is later in the day it can lead to a child not wanting to go to bed in the evening.

Night-time can also be more unsettled. The need to walk can cause frustrated dreams which can disturb sleep; it is common for children to shout out or stand up in the cot at night, and children may not return to sleeping through the night until walking is established and well practised.

Waking during the night can be caused by other stresses or an upset in the daily routine: going to new places, visitors coming, or parents going out for the evening. Although it may seem difficult, parents need to try and remain consistent with established bedtime routines and will need to show extra patience and understanding. These can be very unsettling times for children, and they may need to draw on the added support of some form of comforter.
(*See overleaf.*)

🎞 *Picture story*

EMILY *15 months*

After lunch, Emily takes what is now her only nap of the day. She has an established routine at nap times and although she protests, she settles very quickly for a much-needed rest.

MEGAN *12 months* sometimes wakes at night or shouts out.

1 Emily has her thumb in her mouth as her mother, Corinne, takes her unstairs.

2 They enter the bedroom.

3 Corinne and Emily share a short story together.

4 When the story is over Corinne picks Emily up saying, '*You have a nice sleep*'.

5 Emily starts to vocalise as she anticipates what is about to happen...

6 ...and this is confirmed as Corinne puts Emily in her cot.

7 Corinne rolls Emily onto her side.

8 Emily's protests wane, and she soon settles to sleep.

COMFORTERS: ANXIETY, REGRESSION AND STRESS

Some parents are concerned about the use of comforters and feel they should discourage their children from using them. But what do we do to support ourselves when feeling stressed, or when anxious or nervous? We adults have many props we use as comforters: cigarettes, alcohol, chewing gum, stimulants, chocolate, chewing pencils, biting nails and twiddling hair to mention a few. In addition, we are much better able to find support than our children. For example, if separated from a loved one, we can keep in touch by phone, email, or post, and we can carry a photograph as a physical reminder. As independent adults, we rely on all sorts of props to comfort ourselves, so why do we feel that it is wrong for a baby or young child who is still very dependent to have a comforter to use as a support when needed?

Babies in the womb live in a warm, safe environment, yet they will still raise a thumb towards their mouth for comfort: their hands have been recorded making contact with the face and mouth from 14–36 weeks, and thumb-sucking as early as 24 weeks. Following birth, hands remain very

important to babies, who will suck on them to draw upon their own resources for comfort and support. An older baby will be able to find his or her fist, thumb or finger on their own, which is a valuable resource if they wake up at night and a perfectly natural way for them to self-support.

A soother or dummy serves the same function but can become separated from the child, leaving babies dependent on others to replace it, especially at night. Additional comforters can be in the form of a blanket, a silky label, a piece of cloth, a furry animal, or an imaginary friend, which will be carried around everywhere by the child, adding to their sense of well-being and security.

These different types of comforter are transitional objects of attachment (*see 'Attachments' page 120*); a progression from being dependent to becoming independent, and are far less harmful than some of our adult counterparts. As parents, we may feel we should try to prevent the use of a comforter before it becomes a 'problem' or a 'habit', but this is unlikely to happen in the long term and more likely to increase the need for something else.

Comforters are a healthy and natural way to self-support in times of tiredness, anxiety, stress,

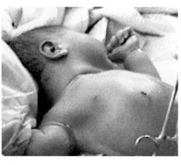

Ethan has just been delivered, and the first thing he does is to put hand to mouth to suck his thumb. (*Picture from* The Social Baby.)

illness and allergies, or when frightened. Children need and enjoy the support they gain from a comforter; if not they wouldn't use them. A child's emotional well-being is all important and it is better not to be overly concerned. In time, the security children gain from their developing social world and peers will lessen their need for this extra support, though a night-time comforter may continue to be used for much longer. It is worth reflecting on the type of comforter we used as a child and the reasons why we stopped.

With an ever-expanding world to explore, children begin to learn that it comes with boundaries and rules. Their need for independence whilst being dependent is often confusing; wanting to do something but not being able to is frustrating. To be separated from someone they depend on, even for a short time, is unsettling and they have to learn to trust that person to return to them.

REGRESSION

These anxieties can be scary, and one way children deal with them is to regress. A child may seem to be making leaps forward in either physical or mental ability, and then suddenly 'go all baby-like again'. Children find accomplishing new tasks and skills very exciting but also quite unnerving; they need time to adjust and assess this latest phase. By taking a step back and revisiting a past, more secure and familar time in their life, and with support, they can develop greater self-esteem and the confidence to make the next step forward.

HANNAH *2 years 4 months* shows that sometimes she feels the need to be fed like 'a baby'.

Some adult comforters are more harmful than those used by children.

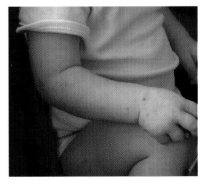

TOM *19 months* has an allergic reation, which becomes worse in stressful situations.

📽 *Picture story*

RUNNING OFF

Wanting independence whilst being dependent

Improving mobility and the need for greater independence makes it very appealing for children to run unrestricted in whatever direction they choose. However, their fearlessness (*see 'Climbing', page 94*) means they are impulsive and unaware of the dangers in 'running off' and away from those they depend upon. This often puts children in the dilemma of needing to be near, but wanting to run off, as can be seen when a child asks to be picked up, but, having allowed this to happen, immediately squirms to get back down.

When children get 'stuck' in this uncertainty, they find it difficult to make the first moves towards resolving it themselves. Parents can help their children by meeting them half way and offering support and empathy.

MONA *16 months*

1 As Nadira opens the front door, Mona is immediately ready to go out of the house.

2 Mona has run to the pavement near the front door and looks back for her mother...

TOM *19 months*

Tom loves to walk by himself but it is late morning and he is tired. He seems to be in a dilemma as to what he wants to do.

1 Tom has become unhappy and his mother, Mandy, offers a supporting hand.

5 Tom stops running and cries. Mandy offers verbal support...

6 ...and decides to walk on a little to give Tom space. He settles, and again Mandy offers a supporting hand. Tom seems unsure what to do.

Mona loves to play outside, and when her mother, Nadira, opens the door, Mona runs out, leaving Nadira no choice but to run after her.

3 ...before running off along the path. Nadira calls Mona back and runs after her.

4 She catches up with Mona...

5 ...and brings her back. Nadira is careful not to turn it into a game.

2 Tom rejects Mandy's hand as he turns and...

3 ...runs from her.

4 As Mandy catches up with Tom, he turns back and runs from her again, vocalising his protest.

7 Mandy walks back towards Tom, offering her hand and empathises with him. As she nears, he hits out at her hand and again becomes upset.

8 Mandy decides to help his uncertainty and scoops him into her arms and kisses him...

9 ...then immediately distracts his attention by talking to him about something in the hedge.

📽 *Picture story*

RESTRICTION

To keep within limits

As the size of 'their world' increases, the need for personal space becomes important to children. Anything we do that impairs their vision or movement, and interferes with their greater need at the time, may not be tolerated.

Everyday activities such as changing a nappy, putting on shoes, a hat, coat or generally getting ready to go out can cause a child to feel restricted and may result in non co-operation.

EMILY *15 months*

1 Emily kicks her legs furiously as Corinne attempts to put her leg in the trousers.

EMIL *20 months*

Every day Emil goes with his mother, Abi, to collect his brother, Henry, from school. Abi has already put on her coat and now it is time for Emil to put on his.

1 Abi has Emil's coat and is about to catch his left arm as he swings around...

2 ...and aims it towards the sleeve of the coat.

6 Emil rolls over again, but his protests are waning...

7 ...and Abi successfully puts his right arm in the coat.

Previously, Emily never minded getting dressed, but now she makes it difficult for her mother, Corinne.

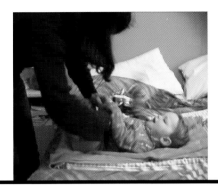

2 Emily becomes vocal and waves her arms as Corinne does up the trousers.

3 Emily arches her back and tries to wriggle from Corinne as she puts on a shoe.

4 Corinne holds Emily firmly as she continues to dress her.

3 Emil realises what is about happen and throws his head back in protest. Abi struggles to keep his arm in the coat sleeve as Emil...

4 ...sinks to the floor...

5 ...turning onto his stomach and shooting out his arm. Abi has skilfully managed to get one arm in the coat and now goes for the other.

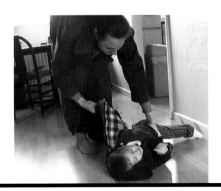

8 Emil tries to turn away from Abi but his struggle is noticeably less...

9 ...enabling Abi to scoop him up...

10 ...and sit down whilst she buttons up Emil's coat with ease. Emil now appears happy at the prospect of going out.

📽 *Picture story*

RESTRAINING

To hold back and to deprive of freedom

To immobilise children when they want their freedom can push them beyond their limits and make them frustrated and unco-operative. Children are very strong for their size and often 'go stiff' if they do not want to be put in a buggy or car seat.

Children of this age do not understand the dangers connected with roads and vehicles; if there is any possiblity of danger, there can be no negotiating, and this can cause conflict.

TOM 19 months

Ever since Tom has learned to walk, he protests strongly when he has to go in his buggy.

JAKE 24 months

Occasionally when Jake and his mother, Sarah, go to the supermarket, she prefers to sit him in the seat of the trolley so she can complete her shopping more quickly. Jake likes the freedom of being able to run around the shop and becomes very upset and unco-operative when Sarah prevents him by putting him in the seat, and so restraining him.

1 Tom happily trots beside his mother, Mandy.

4 ...as he struggles to get free.

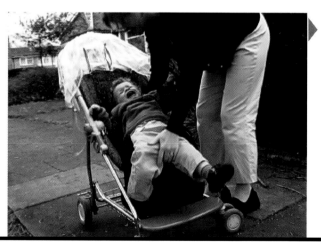

5 Tom's leg flies out as he stiffens his body and screams.

2 As they head towards a busy main road, Mandy scoops Tom up. Tom protests, and kicks Mandy as she explains why she has to put him in the pram.

3 He continues his protest…

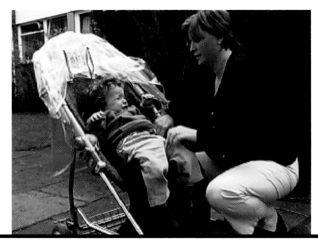

6 Mandy keeps talking calmly to Tom, who is able to calm sufficiently for Mandy to strap him in safely.

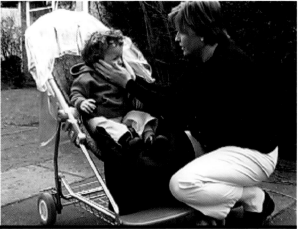

7 Mandy wipes his tears away, empathising with him. She also reinforces the need for him to be in the safety of the pram until he can get out and walk once more.

TANTRUMS: WANTING INDEPENDENCE WHILE BEING DEPENDENT

Tantrums can start to occur at any time during the child's second year, and it is possibly the one pattern of behaviour parents dread most. It is, however, a positive sign that a child is making steps towards becoming an individual independent human being. Tantrums also show us that our children are starting to know their own minds and are developing a desire to take some control over their lives. The difficulty for them at this stage is that they have only limited understanding and self-control.

WHAT IS A TANTRUM?

A tantrum is an immature response by children with a limited ability to process and deal with their emotions in a given situation. Tantrums can be triggered easily by a variety of situations and are brought on by a build-up of frustration or anger when their desires are not met or their new-found need for independence is interrupted.

What can trigger a tantrum?

The nature of tantrums can change as children grow older. For younger children, it is a reaction to a situation, and shows their inability to cope. In older children, it may remain the same or, depending on how the tantrums have been managed in the past, become a negotiating tool to get something they want, or to push/test a boundary. There are many triggers for tantrums, but most fall into the following categories:

Parents
- Not listening.
- Too busy or preoccupied with our own problems to give children time.
- Not always physically being there for them.

Children
- Trying to achieve something for which they don't have the abilities or skills.
- Not being able to convey what they want, or make themselves understood, because they lack the language skills.
- Being unable to get an adult's attention, who may be on the phone, talking with someone, or busy doing something else.
- Testing boundaries or rules.

Children's ability to reason is severely restricted by the fact that they are learning concepts such as time, patience and waiting. They lack concentration, and with limited short-term memory, children have to say what is in their head, or they forget and become frustrated. They live for the here and now, this instant. Children are simply not able, mentally, to stand waiting in a long queue, and the words 'soon', 'in a minute', or 'later' have little or no relative meaning to them other than 'not now'. Similarly, when children are involved in play, to be told, 'Come on, we have to go now' does not make any sense to them (see 'We may be adults but we can still pretend', page 28). Frustration or anger can

JAKE *24 months* does not like supermarket shopping.

build up quickly and is expressed in the only way a child knows: by crying, shouting, screaming, hitting, biting, jumping up and down or throwing themselves on the floor.

Parents and other adults often associate this behaviour with non-compliance. They may then respond to the child in ways that vent their own frustration, displaying similar behaviour to that of the child.

UNDERSTANDING TANTRUMS

How parents help their children through a tantrum becomes an important part of their learning about themselves and the boundaries that exist in their social world. We need to acknowledge that these outbursts are a normal pattern of behaviour and an important step towards independence.

It cannot be emphasised enough how important it is to recognise and understand where children are at this stage of their development. Younger children lack a sense of responsibility for their actions and have few ways to express frustration or anger. They are living in a world which does not yet make complete sense to them. Many events in children's daily lives need to be put in some sort of order. Their limited capacities do not include the skills needed to manage anger or frustration, and on many occasions younger children slip into a tantrum – and out of control. This can be a very frightening experience for them, as children may not be able to make sense of what is happening and quickly forget what triggered it. In this situation they will look to their carers for support. If they see the person they depend on becoming angry with them, the experience becomes even more confusing and frightening. The best way we can help our children is to remain calm and to be consistent.

WORKING THROUGH TANTRUMS WITH YOUNGER CHILDREN
At home...

If the tantrum is in the home, try to allow the child some time and space to self-calm. Offer to meet the child half way for support and a hug, and then distract. Be prepared to be rejected, but keep trying at intervals, as it takes time for children to work through their emotions and become calm. It is probable the child will want to come to you, but cannot make that first step. (See 'Managing a tantrum', page 112.)

When the tantrum is over, try to assess what triggered it, so that next time it may be possible to intervene earlier and prevent one. Ask yourself if your expectations were realistically attainable by the child at that particular moment. By remaining calm, consistent and supportive, parents can encourage and help motivate their child to learn the skills that will enable him or her to overcome what caused the frustration in the first place. Odd as it may seem, helping a child to manage tantrums can help improve their self-control and verbal negotiating skills.

In public...

A tantrum in a public place always seems worse, because it feels as if everyone is looking and every action is being judged, even though they probaby are not. Most people who have had a child will have experienced this and are more likely to sympathise, though this is no comfort when *you* are in the no-win situation. The same principles apply for working the tantrum through, but if it is extreme, the best option may be to pick up your child and take him or her to a different location, away from where the tantrum began. Distracting may then work, as the original trigger will no longer be in view.

If tantrums become regular or difficult to manage, it may be easier to look for alternative ways to avoid the situation in the first place, such as sharing child-care for a couple of hours, so you can each shop without your child, or go with a friend who can help you with him or her, or even speed-shop for fewer things in less time.

If this is not possible, before leaving the house, talk to your child, involving him or her with the activity and explain what is happening and why. Listen to what he or she is saying and try to understand, which can help reduce the child's frustration. Bring distractions with you – a favourite toy or book, a snack or a drink, and introduce them gradually during the time you are out. Praise your child at every opportunity.

TANTRUMS WITH OLDER CHILDREN
Consistency

As children become older, they begin to learn about emotions and start to understand that certain behaviours might help them get the result they are striving for. As language skills improve, children become better able to make themselves understood, but they can still become very distressed if their requests are misunderstood or not met. This can be difficult for parents, who are often put on the spot to make a quick decision, knowing they run the risk of the child having a tantrum if they don't. On these occasions parents may relent in order to avoid a tantrum and *'give them what they want to keep them quiet'*. Unfortunately, this sends a clear signal to the child that this is a good way to achieve what he or she wants, and if on the next occasion the parent does not relent, the child is more likely to have a full-blown tantrum (see *'Boundaries'*, page 48).

Time Out – only from around 2 years onwards

As with younger children, we should always try to remain calm, consistent and use distraction. However, this simple approach may not work if a child becomes violent or aggressive, uses unacceptable language or is repeatedly non compliant. In these extreme circumstances the child can become very agitated and shut out, not listening to any attempts parents may make to communicate. At this point, the child needs a more direct way to help self-calm.

A technique known as *Time Out* is a safe, non-violent way in which to stop conflict instantly in a no-win situation. The child is picked up, and carried to a safe place, where he or she can be left to work through their frustration on their own. This offers both parents and child a short time and space apart. The *Time Out* place should be somewhere safe, that you can hear and, ideally, see what's going on. Suitable places are the bottom step of the stairs, a nominated cooling-off chair or settee, or a quiet room. The child's bedroom should not be used: a bedroom needs to be a safe, happy place, not one associated with anger, frustration and conflict. A *Time Out* or cooling-off place should remain constant, as to change it may cause confusion and make it less effective. The time spent in *Time Out* needs to be as short as possible and one minute per year is a good guide, ie 3 minutes for a 3-year-old. However, it is important that the child becomes calm before ending *Time Out*, so that he or she can be receptive and learn from the experience. Supporting the child too soon can reinforce the original negative behaviour.

Meeting half way

Children who have just experienced a tantrum are likely to be extremely upset, with tears replacing their anger. They may find it difficult to come to a parent and may even be fearful of their response. It is up to us to provide the child with an opportunity to return to a safe, loving environment. The child may not be ready, and reject an approach, but this is temporary and is the child's way of saying they are still angry. Keep listening, and observing, and try again. Children will need reassurance and hugs to show they are still cared for, whatever has happened.

The foot of the stairs is a good location for *Time Out*.

Adults have had much more experience in dealing with their emotions than children have had with theirs. Regardless of how we feel towards the child at this time, to make *Time Out* work we have to create a positive outcome. Forgiving unconditionally, using kind, supportive words, close contact, listening, and empathy with their frustration will help children learn to understand their emotions. It will also help them to become truthful, better able to put their trust in us, and gain a sense of positive self-esteem.

As children get older, their language and communication skills will improve. Giving them the time they need to speak, and listening to what they have to say, without pre-empting or finishing sentences for them, shows we are interested. This can help us gain a better understanding of our children and them of us.

COPING IF IT ALL BECOMES TOO MUCH
Self-management

Parenting is the single most demanding and exhausting job we can take on, often without a break for many years. Parents can experience extremes of emotions swaying from unconditional love, '*I couldn't imagine life without my baby*' to sheer dislike and despair: '*Why are you doing this to me?*' It can be frightening to be in a demanding situation and not in control, or worse, to feel we are losing control, which is much the same as it can be for our children during a tantrum.

Self-management, for us, starts by recognising the cues to our own emotions; what are the signs that we are becoming tense and our stress levels

are rising? Feeling hot, becoming impatient, heart pounding or beating quickly, pressure in the head, gritting teeth and breathing heavily, are all signs that frustration and anger are building.

We all get angry – it is part of our make-up. But it is not always easy to learn how to stop being drawn into a conflict. Walk away and shut the door, take a deep breath and count to 10, reappraise the situation; alternatively ring someone, or take you and your child outside for some space. These are all steps towards calming down and becoming in control again. Once this has been achieved, the next difficult step is to re-establish contact with your child. Children are still learning about emotional development and have limited experience to draw on, so it is likely their feelings will be similar to your own.

Whilst children need us to lead the way in resolving conflict, their short memories mean events are soon forgotten, and they actively look to us for reassurance that life has returned to normal. Being able to admit we were wrong and saying sorry, or showing sadness and being upset, adds depth to a child's emotional experience – a positive asset for children's own relationships with their peers in the future.

For some of us, life can become too much to bear, and no amount of love or good intention is going to work. Fortunately there is now a good deal of help available for parents who feel that they, or their children, are out of control. Parentline 0808 800 2222 offers a 24-hour helpline. Your GP or local clinic should also be able to offer advice.

📽 *Picture story*

MANAGING A TANTRUM (1) *Younger children*

1 Tom points to a radio, which belongs to his sister, Laura. He vocalises to Mandy that he wants it. Mandy says, 'No Tom, it's Laura's.'

2 Tom chooses to ignore Mandy and climbs onto the table to get the radio. Mandy calmly repeats, 'No Tom, it's Laura's,' adding, 'No climbing on the table' as she lifts him off...

3 ...and places him on the floor. Tom protests, vocalising loudly and crying.

7 Tom manages to take some steps towards Mandy. With encouragement and empathy...

8 ...Tom is now able to hug Mandy.

9 But only for a few seconds, before he pulls away and...

13 Tom makes a desperate grab for the toy, snatching it out of Mandy's hand.

14 Tom throws it away, as he cries and shouts out, 'NO.' Mandy does not respond to his action. (Nor would she if he had hit her or bitten her.)

15 By remaining in control herself, Mandy knows she is supporting Tom in his attempts to self-calm. Tom becomes exhausted and...

Tom became frustrated when his mother Mandy misunderstood what he was trying to convey to her, (see 'Misunderstandings', page 38). Although Mandy quickly rectified the situation, Tom continues to find his frustration hard to manage on his own, and needs extra support from Mandy.

4 He runs off, screaming.

5 Mandy crouches down a little way from Tom and watches. She gives him some space and lets him try to cope with his feelings.

6 When he glances towards her she offers him a supporting hand.

10 ...his tears and anger return. Mandy remains calm and stays near him as she turns her attention to the toy basket.

11 In order to distract Tom, Mandy selects some possible toys they can play with together. Tom begins to calm and...

12 ...his crying momentarily stops when Mandy says, 'Oh! Look what I've found.'

16 ...sinks into Mandy's lap. She wipes his tears away as she empathises with him.

17 Mandy then introduces another toy, about which Tom vocalises at first, but Mandy remains enthusiastic.

18 She ignores his slight protest and uses the pop-up toy to distract him. Tom settles down and joins in. In less than 3 minutes Tom is smiling and happy again.

🎥 *Picture story*
MANAGING A TANTRUM (2) *Older children*

CARA *3 years 1 month,*
RHIANNON *8 years, sister,*
HANNAH *8 years*

1 Ceri asks Cara to come and sit down and have something to eat. Cara replies, *'No.'*

2 Ceri would prefer to feed all the children together and knows that Cara will be hungry before bedtime. Ceri lifts Cara into the chair. Cara says, *'I'm not hungry.'*

3 She leaps from the chair and hugs Ceri's legs, repeating, *'I'm not hungry.'* Ceri tries again: *'Have something before bed?'* Cara says, *'It's not bedtime.'*

7 Cara then screams after Ceri, *'No don't. Don't put it on. Off.'* Ceri replies, *'You need a bath, you're all sandy.'* Cara squeals as she pinches Ceri, *'No I don't. Turn it off.'*

8 Ceri ignores Cara's actions and squats down; she calmly explains to Cara again why they all need a bath.

9 Cara rejects Ceri's reasons and says, *'Don't.'* She runs off…

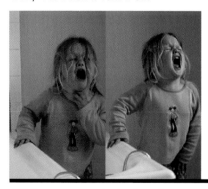

13 Cara goes to the bath and screams out: *'Put it cold.'* To emphasise her frustration even more, she screams as loud as she is able, *'C–O–L–D.'*

14 Cara then runs towards Ceri with her arm raised, and hits Ceri as she screams, *'Put the bath cold.'* Ceri calmly says, *'No hitting mummy.'*

15 Ceri suggests Cara finds some toys to put in the bath. *'No.'* Ceri decides to ignore Cara's protests, and to end her negotiation. She leaves to call the girls.

Cara, her family and friends have been playing on the beach and swimming in the sea. They have come home for tea and a bath, but Cara refuses to eat and quickly slips into a tantrum. The reason for her upset and frustration is seemingly without any clear explanation and her mother, Ceri, tries everything to understand. Ceri does extremely well to remain calm and consistent whilst helping Cara work through the tantrum.

4 Ceri decides to go and run the bath and invites Cara to come and help her. Cara shouts, 'No.' and pulls at Ceri's arm.

5 Ceri calmly says, '*Come on.*' Cara hangs on to her arm…

6 …but lets go as Ceri makes her way upstairs. Cara reaches out and screams her protest.

10 …but immediately returns to Ceri's side.

11 Ceri tries to calm her, but Cara cries, turning her back on her mother as she shrugs Ceri away.

12 Ceri decides to walk away for a moment to give Cara some space. Cara quietens briefly as she watches Ceri.

16 The girls are in the bedroom playing on the computer. Ceri asks them to get ready for the bath. Cara has quietened as she follows Ceri.

17 Rhiannon does want not to be filmed changing, and she peeps out from behind the door. Rhiannon and Hannah share the moment with Cara.

18 Cara's frustration goes as quickly as it came, and she plays happily in the bath. Ceri's reassuring hand shows Cara that she can rely on her mother's support during difficult times.

📽 *Picture story*
HELPING STEPS TO INDEPENDENCE

Children can be encouraged to help themselves become independent. One way is to involve them, especially when getting dressed. This helps reduce their frustration and promotes a sense of achievement.

EMILY *16 months*

Emily is now beginning to anticipate what is going to happen next. She is eager to help when she is undressed by her mother, Corinne.

1 As Corinne unpops Emily's vest, her hands shoot up to take hold of her jumper…

2 …pulling it up towards her face before Corinne has sat her up.

TOM *19 months*

When it is time to go out, Tom is keen to put on his shoes.

1 Tom is sitting on his mother Mandy's lap, attempting to put on his left shoe…

2 …but he decides to drop the shoe on the floor.

5 …and throws it on the floor too.

6 Tom holds onto the sofa to balance himself. Pointing his toe, he judges precisely the distance he needs to enable his foot to go into the shoe.

3 Corinne assists Emily as she vocalises her frustration… her head is stuck.

4 When Emily's head is freed she continues to help remove the garments.

5 Emily vocalises her pleasure and Corinne praises her achievement.

3 Mandy lets Tom climb down and sit on the floor, where he successfully manages to put the shoe on his foot.

4 Tom shares in his success with Mandy. He then takes the right shoe…

7 Tom vocalises to Mandy he is having difficulty. She kneels down in case Tom should need her assistance.

8 Tom shows Mandy he does, and she helps by securing the strap.

9 Triumphant, Tom dances to show his delight at his achievement.

RELATIONSHIPS: WITH MEMBERS OF THE FAMILY, CARERS AND OTHERS

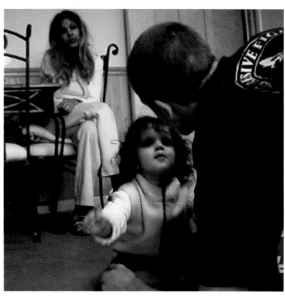

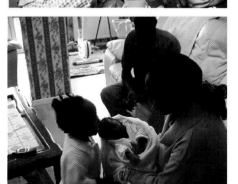

ATTACHMENTS

The most vulnerable time for babies, being completely dependent, is when they are born, and they have the best chance of survival if they are able to bond with a person who can meet their needs. Small babies cry in order to be cared for; their large eyes and smiles are designed to be a powerful magnet for mothers, who in return provide their child with security, food, care and love. When babies come to learn they can rely completely on at least one person for their physical and mental needs, they form what is known as a 'secure attachment', which is based on very early experience, and remains for life. This person becomes their prime carer and is usually, but by no means has to be, their mother.

Babies who do not make this attachment are more likely to have emotional and social difficulties in the future. They will not be secure in the knowledge that they have at least one person they can be completely reliant upon and will develop what is known as an 'insecure attachment'. They may grow to feel they do not deserve the attention that they crave from their parents. When distressed, 'insecurely attached' children may not look to their prime carer for comfort, as they do not feel able to express their emotions openly. They are likely to become introverted as they try to deal with their feelings of anxiety, fear and stress on their own, having learned from experience that these emotions are not met with adequate comfort and support from those they turn to. With a limited ability to manage their emotions without the support of others, children with insecure attachments are likely to feel angry and frustrated and develop patterns of negative behaviour. They will also learn to become self-reliant and in time will intially reject the efforts of those who attempt to help and support them.

One of the ways children develop and improve a secure attachment is to test continually the strength of attachment. Unfortunately, this is why it would appear that the prime carer is often the one who is treated the hardest by the child. It is also why it is important for carers to understand what is happening at this time. Testing can take any number of forms such as biting, kicking, pulling hair, clinging on and unacceptable behaviour, which doesn't seem to happen in the child's relationships with other non-prime carers. This can be a difficult time for the prime carer as it can challenge the feelings they have for their children and also put a strain on the relationship with their partner and other family members.

Children need to know the level of security they can rely upon in the relationship with their prime carer – and its predictability. However, no one person can be the provider of everything a child needs, and it is equally important for the child to learn that certain needs can be met by people other than his or her prime carer. In fact, a child can form close bonds with a number of people.

Children draw on early experiences throughout their lives when forming new relationships, and this includes (in time) their own babies. With secure foundations, children can explore the world with confidence.

(See also 'Relationships: child minders and carers', page 248; 'Comforters', page 100.)

4 As soon as Sapphire hears Zoë's voice, she vocalises and gestures again.

⚏ *Picture story*

DEVELOPING A SECURE ATTACHMENT

SAPPHIRE *14 months*

Sapphire's twin brother, Hugo, can walk, but she is not yet able to, and so is dependent on her mother, Zoë. Zoë leaves Sapphire and goes to the house for a minute. Despite Sapphire making it clear she disapproves of her mother's decision to leave, she is able to cope well, though remaining unsettled until her mother returns. Sapphire shows that she is becoming secure in her attachment, and that she can begin to believe that her mother will return.

1 As Zoë goes to the house, Sapphire immediately vocalises and gestures for her mother to come back. Hugo, who can walk, follows his mother.

2 Alone, and unable to walk, Sapphire can only wait. She looks around and appears calm, but not settled.

3 Sapphire looks around when Emily's mother, Corinne, comes out of the house with Hugo.

5 As Zoë returns, Sapphire calms…

6 …and they play happily together. Sapphire's belief that her mother would return has been confirmed, strengthening her attachment.

📽 *Picture story*

TESTING THE STRENGTH OF ATTACHMENT

Not all children show physical aggression, but it may happen with 1–2½ year olds, and it is a concern for parents. These are not malicious acts, but an impulsive and immature response to a situation. Children of this age have quite a limited ability to comprehend their emotions, and ones as intense as love, excitement or even frustration, may trigger a bite as they attempt to find ways to express their feelings. At this time they are also 'self-centred' with a limited concept of any world beyond their own, so they may not know that when they bite, hit and so on, it hurts.

For example, biting has a close association with food – one of a child's strongest senses of reassurance and comfort from birth. Biting a loved one when excited may link the pleasure of food with feelings of pleasure towards another. However, it is important to make children aware that any aggressive behaviour is not an acceptable way to express feelings.

EMILY *15 months,*
Siblings MEGAN *8 years,* OLIVER *6 years*

Emily has recently started biting her mother, Corinne, who is Emily's prime carer. Corinne did not experience this with her other two children, and she is concerned in case Emily bites her sister and brother and other friends. Corinne has noticed that Emily bites only her and not her father, Rick, and that she bites only when she becomes frustrated or excited, so Corinne is already beginning to anticipate what triggers Emily's biting.

Corinne is using ignoring as a strategy to help Emily learn that biting is not an acceptable way to show excitement. In time, and with consistent support, Emily will be better able to cope with her feelings.

1 After tea, Oliver, Megan and Emily play together. Their games are loud and boisterous; Emily joins in happily.

4 ...still with a neutral gaze and calm voice, Corinne repeats, 'No biting, no biting...'

7 Despite Emily's efforts to engage with her mother, Corinne remains neutral and, still not looking at Emily, puts her down.

2 Megan gives Emily to her mother, Corinne, and Emily bites her shoulder. It clearly hurts and Corinne cries out in pain, 'Ow.'

3 Although it is painful, Corinne is calm and lifts Emily from her shoulder. She gains eye contact and says, 'Don't bite, don't bite.'

5 Emily breaks eye contact and looks away.

6 Megan speaks to her mother, and Emily tries to regain Corinne's attention.

8 This is not the response that Emily wanted and she walks away repeating to herself 'No... nno... nno... no.'

9 Emily does not yet understand the meaning of the word 'no', but from her response to Corinne, she shows that she is beginning to understand it is not acceptable for her to bite.

■ *Picture story*

THE NEED TO BE NEAR

Children can find it difficult to be separated from their prime carer, even for a short time. They need to check that she or he is still near and may call out or do something they know is unacceptable, to make sure of their return.

EMILY *15 months*

Emily's mother, Corinne, goes upstairs to check on the older children. Emily has been absorbed playing in the kitchen near her mother, but she is soon to face a dilemma. Emily knows she is not allowed to go up the stairs by herself but she wants her mother back. She is unsure if she should climb the stairs or not.

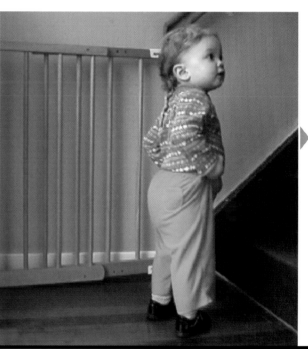

3 Emily continues to play briefly, but when she realises her mother has gone...

4 ...she goes to the bottom of the stairs. Emily can hear Corinne upstairs, talking, and becomes increasingly unsettled, pulling at her clothes.

OPHELIA *18 months*

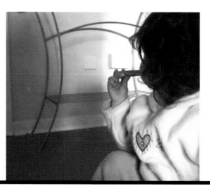

1 Ophelia is playing happily on the floor.

2 She turns as she hears her mother, Melanie, coming.

3 As Melanie passes, Ophelia immediately starts to get up...

1 Corinne touches Emily's head to check she is happy…

2 …before she leaves the kitchen to go upstairs.

5 Emily starts to climb the stairs as soon as she sees her mother coming down, and vocalises to her.

6 Corinne picks up Emily and together they return to the kitchen, to resume what they were doing.

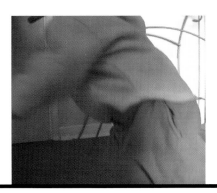

4 …and follows her mother…

5 …into the kitchen.

6 Ophelia now plays with the fridge magnets in the kitchen, near Melanie.

📽 *Picture story*

SEPARATION AND REUNION (1)

Leaving

When parents have to leave their child, for whatever reason, it is emotionally difficult for the child. It can be equally heart-wrenching for the parent, if they are confronted with having to leave a tearful and upset child.

Adults learn to cope with these feelings and are often able to disguise them bravely with a cheery, *'See you later'*. But children who are still trying to understand these raw emotions, will openly display their feelings and dissolve into tears.

It can be of some reassurance to parents to know that the tears and upset are almost always short-lived.

TOM *19 months*

1 Dave goes into the kitchen to get ready to go to work. Tom sees his father...

5 ...and a reassuring rub on the head.

6 Tom's mother, Mandy, comes to see Dave off to work. Tom goes to the door.

7 While Mandy finds something for Dave, Tom goes to his coat...

11 As his father leaves, Tom is gently held back by Mandy. Tom cries out in protest to Dave.

12 With the door closed, and his father gone, Tom looks to Mandy for a response.

13 As Tom crumbles, Mandy offers him a supporting hand.

Tom gets very upset when his father, Dave, leaves for work. Even though it is an established part of the daily routine, Tom always tries to go with him and crumples into tears as Dave leaves.

2 ...and runs into the kitchen to join him.

3 Tom reaches up towards Dave...

4 ...who responds with a kiss...

8 ...and pulls at it.

9 Realising his father is now leaving, Tom lets go of the coat...

10 ...and heads for the door to try and go with Dave. Dave says goodbye.

14 Mandy diverts Tom's attention by suggesting they look at a book together.

15 Tom puts up no resistance, but remains upset.

16 However, Tom settles happily in less than a minute.

📽 *Picture story*

SEPARATION AND REUNION (2)

Making decisions about leaving

As children come to understand they are able to have choices, they want to make the decision on leave-taking; they can leave a parent but a parent cannot leave them.

MONA *16 months*

Mona gets very upset when anyone leaves the house. However, Mona is perfectly happy if she makes the decision to say goodbye, even when it is to her father.

3 As Mona turns to go, her mother, Nadira, also waves goodbye.

4 Nadira takes hold of Mona's hand and they go on their way.

RETURNING FROM WORK

JAKE *24 months*

Each weekday, Jake eagerly awaits the return of his father, Mark, who arrives home from work shortly before Jake goes to bed.

1 As Jake and his mother, Sarah, enjoy a book together, Jake hears the keys in the front door. He points excitedly and says, 'Daddy.'

2 Jake is immediately on his feet and runs towards the door.

1 Mona wants to go out and waves to her father, Youssef.

2 Youssef smiles and waves goodbye to Mona through the window.

5 Later, as we are about to leave. Mona holds her arms out; she does not want us to go.

6 She becomes upset and vocalises her disapproval.

3 Jake leaps at his father, Mark, and he gives him a welcome hug.

4 Mark and Jake kiss as Sarah looks on.

5 Jake remains settled in Mark's arms as Mark and Sarah catch up on the day's events.

FATHERS: A SPECIAL ROLE

A child's relationship with each parent is different, and what they offer the child is of equal value. Fathers who are not prime carers usually have less time with their child and may spend long hours away from them. However, this does not mean the child has less of a bond with the father than with the mother, and studies show that children form very similar attachments with both parents regardless of the amount of time spent together.

What is important for the child is the quality of interaction. Fathers can offer play, fun, stimulation and sensitivity through various activities, such as robust and physical 'rough and tumble' or chasing games, as well as becoming involved with everyday routines such as bath-time, story-time and bedtime.

📽 *Picture story*
MONA *16 months*
Mona loves to run and dive at her father, Youssef.

3 ...until the last moment when he catches Mona as she dives...

OPHELIA *20 months*

When Ophelia's father, Daniel, gets home from work. he enjoys spending time with Ophelia. They enjoy active games such as 'I'm going to eat your toes...', and 'I'll chase you...', before tea, a book, bath and bed.

1 As Mona's mother, Nadira, leads her into the room, Mona can hear her father calling. Her face lights up…

2 …and she runs towards him. Youssef opens his eyes wide as he says, *'Ooh!'* His arms remain by his legs…

4 …and he lifts her…

5 …high above his head. They both share the delight of the game.

📽 *Picture story*

BATH-TIME

A fun time to play and learn together

Most children love playing in the bath, and it provides a good opportunity to share some close time together.

1 Ophelia tries to get into the bath but Daniel stops her and reminds her that the water could be too hot.

5 Daniel blows some bubbles from his hand…

9 …Daniel takes her cue and joins in.

10 Then they play catching the ball.

11 Next, Daniel encourages Ophelia to wash herself.

Ophelia loves bath-time with her father, Daniel.

2 He distracts Ophelia by asking her to, '*Scratch daddy's back after a hard day at work.*'

3 After making sure the temperature of the bath water is safe, Daniel lifts Ophelia into the bath.

4 Ophelia is fascinated by pouring water.

6 ...and Ophelia watches as he blows the bubbles from her hand.

7 Ophelia investigates the water using her tongue.

8 She then instigates a mouth-popping game...

12 Then to remove the plug and put it on the side...

13 ...she does this and claps herself, showing she is beginning to learn to praise herself.

14 Finally they say, '*Bye bye,*' to the bath water before Daniel lifts Ophelia out.

OTHER FAMILY MEMBERS AND CARERS

Children can form close bonds with other members of the family, as well as their carers. These strong attachments give children added security. It also allows them to experience a range of different social interactions and provides an introduction to the many different rules and boundaries which exist in other people's lives.

Children spend a lot of time with their carers, and share many experiences with them. These relationships become extremely special, making carers an important part of the family unit.

A NEW FAMILY MEMBER

When a new member of the family comes along, the family's dynamics can become upset. Children who are not yet able to share – either toys or parents – are now in a situation where they have no choice. They may not be able to understand fully this new situation or the emotions they feel. By respecting, empathising and listening to children, many fears and uncertainties can be allayed, enabling them to remain feeling secure within the family unit. For example, children can become jealous and feel lonely or left out when people's attention turns towards a new baby or when they start nursery, leaving parents and baby alone together. Children may show their emotional uncertainty by regressing to an earlier, more secure time (*see 'Regression', page 101*) when there was no competition from a new baby.

Children can be helped through this time by involving them in the pregnancy and then encouraging them to become part of the new baby's world. Letting them help choose clothes and toys, pushing the pram and so on means they can contribute physically to the baby's care, giving them an opportunity to be included in conversations with other people about the new baby. However, parents also need to build a special time into the daily routine when they can be on their own with the older child without distractions. This allows time for parents to be together and listen to the older child, and to discuss any problems they may have.

At first, children may not like their new brother or sister: sibling rivalry is common in new relationships. If helped sympathetically, the experience can become a positive way for children to begin to find out about and accept the other person. Parents can help by being consistent and remembering that there is one rule for all. In times of disputes between children where the parents have not actually witnessed the incident, protests about 'who hit whom' or 'who said what', cannot be used to coerce parents into taking sides. Encouraging communication will help older children to sort it out themselves.

All children are individuals and although one child may be better at one thing than the other, there will always be something to praise and be proud of in every child. Make them feel an equal and special member of the family, valued for their achievements, rather than being compared with one other.

📽 *Picture story*

1 Olivia's mother, Mary, encourages Olivia to sit and watch Liz as she carries out Alicia's 3-week check.

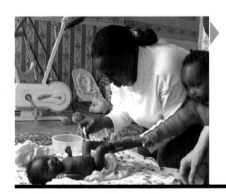

5 As Mary wipes Alicia, Olivia moves round and reaches out to help.

9 Olivia says, 'Baby'....

OLIVIA *20 months*

Liz, a Health Visitor, comes to check the progress of Olivia's baby sister, Alicia, at 3 and 6 weeks.

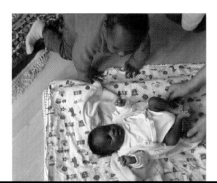

2 Olivia nears her sister as Liz begins to undress Alicia.

3 Olivia peers at her sister…

4 …and then at her mother, as Liz talks.

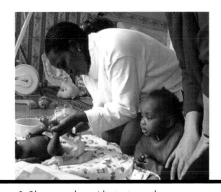

6 She watches Alicia intently as Mary cleans her.

7 Olivia moves so that she can see her sister as she is dressed.

8 At the 6-week check, Alicia is sleeping. Liz takes the opportunity to talk to Alicia's parents, Fred and Mary, and ask if they have anything they would like to ask her. Olivia points out her sister to Liz.

10 …and as Fred comes to stroke Alicia's hand, Olivia also wants to hold his hand.

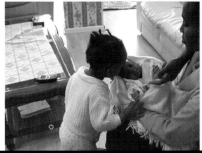

11 She then kisses her sister gently on the forehead.

12 Olivia shows the beginnings of building a relationship with her sister.

📽 *Picture story*

STRANGERS

Sensitivity concerning strangers

Strangers or unfamiliar people can be threatening or even frightening to children of this age, and they may run and cling to their parents for support. Only when they feel secure can children feel confident to look at the stranger.

EMILY *15 months*

A friend of Emily's mother, Corinne, has come to visit. She is unfamilar to Emily.

1 When the door is opened, Emily looks at the new face. She waits for a moment before...

4 Once inside the house, Corinne's attention is focused on her friend as they chat together. Emily becomes unsettled, she looks up to the friend, pulling at her own clothes.

5 She looks down...

8 She runs to Corinne and clings to her legs, burying her head. Corinne strokes her head reassuringly.

9 As Corinne's hands touch her waist, Emily immediately releases her grip, relaxes and puts her arms up, predicting what will happen next.

2 ...looking towards Corinne and ...

3 ...making contact with her. Emily is now able to look at the stranger again.

6 ...then up to her mother.

7 Emily flings out her arms to gesture her need for contact with her mother.

10 She is not disappointed, and now secure in her mother's arms, Emily is able to slowly survey the stranger's face.

11 Still unsure, she regains eye contact with Corinne and uses her thumb to give her extra support.

🎥 Picture story
OTHER CHILDREN

Children of this age are 'self-centred' and are learning to understand the concept that others have 'selves' of their own. They assume that what they see is theirs (see 'Favourite words', page 156).

This makes the concept of sharing extremely hard for children to understand (see 'Playing with other children', page 206). Sharing their space and the attention of the prime carer (upon whom they depend for their security), is even harder for them to comprehend. This can be too threatening and may not be tolerated.

EMILY *17 months*

Emily's mother, Corinne, has invited her friend, Zoë, and the twins to play. As Corinne shuts the door and chats to her guests, Emily shows she is feeling vulnerable.

TOM *20 months,*
KATHERINE *3 years 6 months*

Tom's mother, Mandy, often looks after Katherine while her mother is at work. Katherine is a quiet, sensitive girl and she and Tom play well together. But as soon as Katherine and Mandy have a cuddle or a close moment, Tom shows his disapproval. Tom was playing happily when he looked up and saw Katherine sitting on his mother's lap.

1 Tom stops playing, and immediately becomes upset. Vocalising loudly, he starts to run towards them.

2 He tries to push Katherine off, but he is unsuccessful.

3 Then he raises his arm...

4 ...and hits Katherine. Mandy says, 'No, Tom' and suggests there is room for them both on her lap.

5 Katherine is unconcerned by Tom's actions and ignores them. Mandy praises Katherine for her tolerance to Tom, who climbs up to join them.

1 Emily finds herself separated from her mother. She has her thumb in her mouth for support.

2 She moves nearer to Corinne and pulls at her dress, showing she feels unsure.

3 As Corinne passes by, Emily grabs her mother's leg. She laughs with joy and relief as they are reunited once again.

6 Tom's tears have turned instantly to a happy smile as he regains contact with his mother.

COMMUNICATION: LISTENING AND LANGUAGE

Our ability to speak to one another makes humans unique. It enables us to express our feelings, say what we want, describe what we see and imagine. Listening to another gives us the opportunity to learn, to change the way we think, and to see the world from a number of different points of view.

Babies are born 'totally international' with the ability to differentiate between one language and another. They hear individual sounds that make up words and always have a preference for their native tongue. At this early age babies have their greatest potential to learn any language; by their teens this natural ability has been lost.

POINTING, VOCALISING AND LOOKING

Getting attention with limited or no language skills

In order to gain the attention of a parent, children start to give clear signs of communication by either pointing, being vocally persistent, looking intently, or a combination of the three.

Pointing out things they see around them, and having a parent name the object, enables children to learn that each object has a particular sound pattern linked to it. By repeatedly pointing out the object and having it named, the image which is represented by that word will become held in the child's mind without having to have the physical object in front of him or her.

As the child's language skills develop, the use of gestures becomes more evident and plays an important role in enhancing communication. However, if the child is ignored or misinterpreted, it can lead to frustration. (*See 'How we use language', page 38.*)

⚫⚫ 🎞 *Picture story*   ▶

EMILY *15 months*

Emily breaks from a moment with her mother, Corinne, when she spots something out of the window.

EMILY *15 months*

1 From previous experience, Emily has learned that raisins are kept in a cupboard in the kitchen. Emily vocalises to her mother, Corinne, and points to the cupboard.

EMIL *20 months*

While in his mother's arms, Emil remembers an exciting story to tell us. The other day he saw a fire engine across the street. Although he is able to use more words than Emily, he also uses emphatic hand gestures to make himself understood better.

1 Emil excitedly points and looks out of the window saying, '*Fire.*' His parents, Abi and Jack, help Emil as he tells his story by filling in the gaps.

2 Emil points to us...

1 Emily enjoys a quiet moment with her mother, Corinne.

2 Something has caught Emily's attention. She vocalises and points, alerting Corinne to follow her finger and gaze.

3 Corinne turns to look out of the window. Emily can now share what she has seen with her mother. Corinne says, 'Bird...'

Emily is able to go to the kitchen and show her mother, Corinne, exactly what she would like. At the moment she is reliant on Corinne to get it for her.

2 The cupboard is high up on the wall, beyond her reach.

3 She moves into the kitchen and gazes up intently at the cupboard, emphasising what she would like.

4 Corinne gets the jar of raisins from the cupboard. Emily has shown her mother what she wants and this time she has been successful.

3 ...outstretches his hand...

4 ...and closes it again, gesturing us to 'come and see.'

5 Emil once again points out of the window, directing us to look in that direction, saying, 'Fire.'

📷 *Picture story*
LISTENING, UNDERSTANDING AND FOLLOWING AN INSTRUCTION

Children of this age can follow simple instructions. They can be helped to succeed by using the child's name to get his or her atttention; then by asking one clear instruction, making sure that the request is attainable for the child.

Children have short memories and are easily distracted and can change their interest very quickly. If the child has difficulties, help him or her to succeed and re-assess if the request was too hard.

EMILY *15 months*

Emily shows her mother, Corinne, that she has listened and understood an instruction and can follow it through.

1 Emily is alert, not distracted by another activity and is ready to listen to her mother. Corinne asks slowly and clearly, '*Emily, go and get your push-along-duck, please.*'

5 ...and finds the push-along toy.

WAVING WHEN ASKED AND WAVING SPONTANEOUSLY

Children copy and repeat adult gestures from an early age. The reponses they receive help them learn appropriate social behaviour. From birth, adults smile at babies, and babies grow to learn that if they smile at adults, adults in turn smile back. Waving hello and goodbye is a similarly learned social gesture and during the second year a child will at first wave when asked and later wave spontaneously. Smiling and waving is twice as rewarding for both child and adult.

When asked to wave goodbye by her mother, EMILY *17 months* rotates her hand and accompanies her wave with her special new smile.

2 Corinne waits a moment, checking to see if Emily has heard. Corinne repeats the request...

3 ...and repeats the instruction once more. Emily has had time to process what has been said to her and this time she leaves her mother's side.

4 She goes towards the toy basket...

6 Emily hurries back, carrying the toy. Her eyes are fixed on the floor about two metres ahead of her; she is not yet practised in running and will find any obstacles difficult to negotiate.

7 Emily has done well not to get distracted by the other toys she came across in the basket.

8 Corinne greets Emily's return with a smile and praises her success.

OPHELIA *18 months* is familiar with 'hello' and 'goodbye'. As soon as anyone says, '*Goodbye, Ophelia,*' she will spontaneously smile and wave.

📽 *Picture story*   EMILY *15 months* ▶

THE WORLD OF SYMBOLS

The importance of picture books, the written word and drawing

Our world is made up of three-dimensional objects that can be seen. Some can be touched, some eaten, and some are able to move – by themselves or mechanically.

Objects can be portrayed two-dimensionally in many different ways, as pictures and words; photographs and illustrations may be true to life or abstract, varying in size and colour.

Objects also have a spoken sound pattern which is represented in two-dimensions by a symbol in the form of a word. Words are made up of a combination of other symbols (letters).

Children need to be able to make sense of this. Looking at pictures, the symbols that make up words, and hearing the sound pattern attached to them, helps children to link the three.

3 Emily points to a leaf. Corinne again tells Emily its name.

DRAWING   EMIL *20 months*

Children's 'scribble' may appear meaningless, but these marks are the beginnings of pictures and symbols. They help hand/eye co-ordination and use of the preferred hand. Children can discover the properties of different materials (paper, sand, food) with the various tools used (crayons, paints, sticks, fingers).

1 Emil and his mother Abi are sitting, ready to draw. Abi encourages Emil to draw on the paper.

2 Emil draws in circular movements.

1 Emily is sitting on her mother Corinne's knee, ready to look at a book together. They both enjoy this close shared activity.

2 Corinne points to an animal on the page and tells Emily, '*Dog. A dog goes,* woof woof.'

4 Emily turns the pages to find a familar picture of an animal…

5 …she points and attempts to make the sound the animal makes. Corinne confirms this for her by joining in.

3 Abi asks Emil what he is drawing. He says, '*Reema*' (his elder sister).

4 Abi writes 'Reema' at the top of the paper.

5 Emil points and says, '*Reema.*' He has started to notice that marks can represent symbols which relate to his sister's name.

CATEGORISING

Categorising: *putting into a class or a division; grouping a number of items considered as a collective unit.*

Once children have learned the names of different objects, they can begin to learn the more difficult concept of how to categorise them. A child will be able to distinguish a dog from a chair based on its physical appearance, and that one is living (it moves), and the other is not (it does not move).

Early attempts to categorise result in objects being placed in large groups. Children have yet to learn, for example, that not all four-legged animals are called 'dog', and so may also call a cat or a cow 'dog'. Other examples of children making early mistakes categorising are when they refer to: all men as 'daddy'; all round objects as 'ball'; all drinks as 'tea'; and all colours as 'blue'. Given time, experience and repetition, they will learn how to categorise into smaller groups.

A child may also be able to distinguish between something that is alive and moves, and something else that is not alive, yet also moves. At this stage it does not mean the child has an understanding of what is living and what is mechanical, or what the difference signifies.

TOM *19 months* points to Clive and says, '*Daddy.*'

TOM *19 months* and OPHELIA *18 months* can recognise a real plane and bird as objects that both fly, and they are starting to be able to relate their movements to miniature toys. They have not yet learned that one is living and one is not.

TOM *19 months* holds small models of a plane and a bird. As he pushes the plane along his leg, he makes 'wooshing' sounds.

1 OLIVIA *20 months* points to her mother, Mary, on the TV screen, which is showing a video of her family and says, 'Mummy'...

2 ...but she also points and says, 'Mummy,' when she sees Helen on the screen.

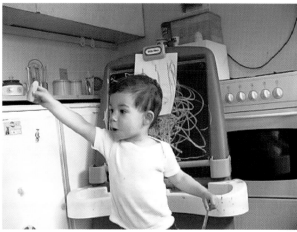

EMIL *20 months* is familar with his neighbour's dog. He now refers to all four-legged animals he meets as 'Dog.'

When JAKE *24 months* is asked what colour his yellow chalk is, he holds it out and says, 'Blue.'

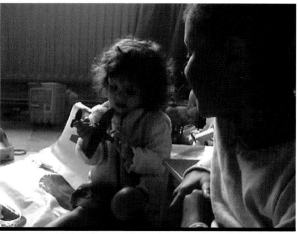

1 OPHELIA *18 months* moves the bird up and down, making the wings flap...

2 ...and with her finger winds the propellor of the plane, showing she is aware it is mechanical.

📽 *Picture story*

EMILY *15 months*

RHYMES, RHYTHM AND SONG (1)

Learning language and sociability through rhymes, rhythm and song

The tone of adult conversation is usually a steady drone, but when parents help their children to learn language, they become natural teachers. They speak in a higher tone, using a sing-song voice and well-pronounced words (known as motherese). This not only holds the child's attention but makes it easier for the child to process words. By emphasising the 'ee's', 'aah's' and 'oo's', slowing down speech, and breaking up the sound patterns of words, parents help their child to see what shapes the mouth and tongue have to make in order to produce a particular sound. The repetition and rhythm of nursery rhymes and songs enhances these language skills.

1 Corinne is asking Emily to find a nursery rhyme she would like them both to sing.

5 Emily's head goes forward...

6 ...and back...

7 ...and forward again, in time to the rhythm of the rhyme.

EMIL *20 months*

Emil and his mother, Abi, sing 'Twinkle Twinkle Little Star' together as they watch it played on TV.

1 While the song is playing on the TV, Abi joins Emil on the chair. Emil watches how Abi makes a star with her hands and tries to copy.

Emily and her mother, Corinne, enjoy the nursery rhyme, 'Baah, Baah, Black Sheep' together.

2 On turning the page, Emily spots a favourite, and has started the rhyme 'B...

3 ...aah'...

4 Corinne joins in, and as she does so...

8 Emily points to the picture and Corinne says 'sh...

9 ...e...e...p,' as Emily checks Corinne's mouth shape.

10 Emily shows Corinne she has had enough and her foot comes up to push the book away.

2 He enthusiastically copies the actions, even though he cannot sing all the words of the song.

3 The moment is made more special because Abi has joined in with the song.

Picture story

RHYMES, RHYTHM AND SONG (2)

'Pat-a-cake'

Many rhymes give the opportunity for hand, face and eye contact, giving children a better opportunity to see, hear, copy and have physical contact with their parents. The rhymes sometimes give way to other forms of play.

Children enjoy clapping, not only in recognition of an achievement but also to enhance their rhythm as they clap and sing along to songs.

OPHELIA *18 months*

Ophelia and her mother, Melanie, play 'Pat-a-cake'. They have played the rhyme only a few times before, and Ophelia is a little unsure. Another favourite is 'Row, Row, Row your Boat'.

1 Melanie introduces the new rhyme by clapping her hands. At first Ophelia is unsure about what to do…

2 …but then copies her mother.

3 As the rhyme nears the end, Melanie pats Ophelia's tummy, *'Put it in the oven for baby…'*

4 …Ophelia giggles and holds her tummy. She anticipates the start of something more familiar, the tickling game.

5 Melanie takes Ophelia's cue and tickles her tummy as she completes the rhyme, *'…and me.'*

6 They both laugh, their mouths open wide in harmony. Ophelia gets ready for another approach.

7 Ophelias tucks her chin into her chest as her mother spiders her fingers up Ophelia's chest.

8 The final climax of the game is reached as Melanie tickles Ophelia's neck.

9 They both relax, smiling at each other, having enjoyed the moment together.

📽 *Picture story*

RHYMES, RHYTHM AND SONG (3)

'Round and Round the Garden' and 'This Little Piggy'

By observing the tone of voice and facial expressions used, the repetition of rhymes enables children to learn and anticipate what comes next and when. They will often encourage their parents ahead of the game with great excitement. As children get older and become familiar with the rhymes, they love to take turns and practise this skill on their parents.

JAKE *24 months*
Jake has just learned the rhyme 'Round and Round the Garden', but he becomes excited and often finishes ahead of his mother, Sarah.

4 Sarah has just started her turn, when Jake is already at *'one step'* on his own arm.

5 Sarah is now at *'one step'* and Jake *'two steps'*.

THIS LITTLE PIGGY...

1 Jake is not familar with this rhyme and eagerly awaits what Sarah says and does.

2 Jake freezes as Sarah's fingers run up his legs and she says, *'Wee, wee, wee...*

3 *...all the way home!'*

1 Jake has decided to start the rhyme. Although he uses his right finger on Sarah's palm, his left hand is outstretched mirroring that of his mother.

2 *'One step…'*

3 *'…two step and tickle under there.'* Jake takes great delight in making Sarah squeal.

6 As Sarah reaches *'two steps'* Jake has already tickled himself and anticipates the finale.

7 He is not disappointed as Sarah tickles the other side of his neck. They both smile and laugh in harmony enjoying this special moment.

4 Jake requests the rhyme again but this time he helps Sarah by pointing to his own toes.

5 He now attempts to do the actions to Sarah, but without the words.

6 He finishes by running his fingers up her leg. It will not be long before he has learned this rhyme too.

FAVOURITE WORDS (1)

'No' and 'Mine'

In order to become independent, children have to learn to make decisions, good or bad, and develop negotiating skills. They gradually become aware of 'self' and begin to understand that they have minds of their own and that they can make decisions for themselves. This is a positive sign of becoming a unique independent person. The first step is to be able to make choices.

From around 18 months the words 'no' and 'mine' become favourites for children. They will often refuse to do what they are asked and some-times ignore parents completely by apparently going deaf. Children hear the word 'no' and see daily the gestures associated with it used by adults. Now they can say the word 'no' and shake their heads emphatically from side to side, seemingly being stubborn, unco-operative or even 'lying'. (See 'Truthfulness', page 286.)

Although children say 'no', they may not mean 'no'. It is likely they are more concerned to show that they are now able to make a decision. They have not yet learned the true meaning of 'no' or 'yes', and at this age are still trying to make sense of them.

OPHELIA *18 months* shakes her head to say 'No.'

📽 *Picture story*

EMIL *20 months*

Emil's parents, Abi and Jack, have noticed that he says 'No' to everything at the moment, even if it seems obvious the answer should be 'Yes'.

3 Abi offers a replacement. Confused by his feelings, Emil says, *'Yes...no...give me...'* and hits out at the new pen.

6 Emil steps down from the chair to take the picture to his father, Jack.

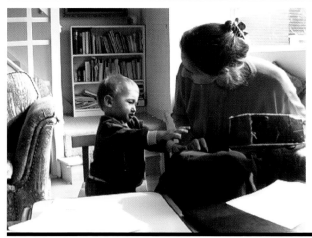

1 Emil has been pretending to eat his crayon. His mother Abi immediately removes both the crayon and the box.

2 Emil demonstrates his frustration by throwing his whole body away from Abi and crying out.

4 Abi quickly distracts Emil by picking up his picture...

5 ...and saying *'Do you want to show papa?'* Smiling, Emil replies, *'No.'*

7 Jack asks him: *'Is this your picture?'* Emil replies, *'No.'*

8 Undeterred by his reply, Jack praises Emil's picture and kisses him.

FAVOURITE WORDS (2)
'No' and 'Mine'

Children of this age are 'self-centred' but they are beginning to learn the concept that others have a 'self' of their own.

Although children say the word 'mine', they may not know the true meaning of the word and are beginning to gain a sense of ownership by the response of those around them. This makes sharing an extremely difficult concept for children of this age.

Picture story

EMIL 20 months

Emil's sister, Reema, has a pet hamster in which Emil shows great interest, but he believes it belongs to him and not Reema.

TOM *19 months* loves wearing his sister Laura's shoes. As he puts on her shoe he repeats, 'Mine, mine'!

1 Emil looks longingly at the cage to see if the hamster is there.

2 He then looks at his mother, Abi.

3 Abi has sat Emil close to the cage and together they look for the hamster. Abi spots the hamster.

4 Emil says, *'Mine.'*

5 Abi replies: *'Oh no, Reema's!'*

6 Abi repeats: *'Reema's hamster.'*

◉ *Picture story*

IGNORING AND GOING DEAF

As children strive towards independence, ignoring can become common, along with '*no*' and '*mine*'. This can be particularly frustrating for parents, but it shows that children are discovering they have a choice whether to do what is asked or not. The question to ask is: is what we are asking them to do important or can we work around it?

EMIL *20 months*

1 Emil is engrossed in his TV programme.

4 Determined not to look round at his father, Emil smiles as Jack again requests a kiss.

5 Jack bends down and turns Emil's head towards him.

8 Jack requests a kiss on the cheek, Emil smiles, leans towards his father, but chooses to remain looking at the TV.

9 Emil looks at where Jack would like a kiss...

2 Jack calls Emil from the top of the stairs. *'Come and give me a kiss.'* Emil turns to look, indicating he has heard.

3 Emil chooses to ignore Jack and his attention returns to the TV. Jack talks to Emil as he nears.

6 He allows Jack to kiss him on the cheek.

7 Emil immediately returns to face the TV.

10 ...but again he ignores the request and shrugs his father away, returning to the TV.

11 Jack respects Emil's decision and decides it is not important now, leaving Emil to watch the TV programme.

LEARNING THROUGH PLAY

Children learn and discover a great deal through play; they learn the basic laws of physics and theories about properties; cause and effect (an object remains still unless pushed), up and down, in and out (a solid object will not pass through another solid object), gravity, and so on. Children are developing the ability to recall past experiences and string all these learned theories together, enabling them to solve new problems.

🎥 *Picture story*

FINDING A HIDDEN TOY

In order to find a hidden object, a child needs to string some strategies together. Putting together a number of skills in the correct sequence is a skill in itself.

EMILY *15 months*

Emily has seen her toy car go underneath the sofa and wants it back so that she is able to continue playing.

Emily has the ability to hold an image of an object in her memory; she can remember, and believes it is still there, even though she cannot see it, which is why she pulls up the cover to grab hold of the toy car.

1 Emily peers under the sofa to see if she can find her toy car.

4 Corinne pulls up the cover and retrieves the car.

7 Emily now grabs the cover...

2 She lifts the cover to get a better view…

3 …but it is not there. She then looks to her mother, Corinne, vocalising her need for help.

5 She places it just under the edge of the sofa, where Emily can now see it.

6 Corinne replaces the sofa cover to hide the car.

8 …reaches under the sofa…

9 …and successfully retrieves the toy car.

SHORT ATTENTION SPAN

Children of this age have a very short attention span and will flit from activity to activity, sometimes spending as little as a minute on any one. Their thirst for new and exciting things to learn about and discover is endless; however, they may repeat the same activity over and over again.

Giving children the opportunity to succeed in a chosen activity may help their concentration and encourage them to complete a task successfully.

Picture story

OPHELIA *18 months*
Ophelia plays a shapes puzzle with her mother, Melanie.

OPHELIA *18 months* finds it hard to keep her concentration on any one thing for very long.

3 Ophelia tries …

4 …Melanie helps her by turning the shape…

1 Melanie and Ophelia begin to play.

2 To help Ophelia, Melanie points to the correctly shaped hole for the piece of puzzle Ophelia is holding.

5 …Ophelia tries again, but still it won't go…

6 …she puts the piece in her mouth, and becomes distracted by something else.

MULTI-SENSORY EXPERIENCES

The sensory experience of sight, sound and touch

A child of this age learns not just by observation but also from sound and touch.

Children bang objects together, hammer them, or shake them to see what noises they make. This enables them to make connections between the action that causes a sound (which they hear but cannot see) and their ability to predict what sound each action will make. Toys can provide purpose-built tools for this, but children also use objects they come across in their daily lives. For example, banging cups together, hitting spoons on the table, throwing something on different floor surfaces to hear the sound it makes on impact.

Children also learn to make connections between sound and touch, by tearing paper and crinkling cellophane, or anything they find. Children need to repeat these actions as many times as necessary for those connections to make sense.

🎥 *Picture story* ▶

OPHELIA 18 months

Ophelia and her mother, Melanie, play with a peg toy. When the coloured pegs are hit with a hammer, they make different sounds. As Ophelia hits a coloured peg she finds each produces a different sound. By repeating the exercise over and over Ophelia is fixing in her mind which colour peg makes which sound. Soon she will be able to predict exactly what noise she will hear when she hits a certain colour peg with the hammer.

JAKE 20 months

Jake likes the sound when he crinkles his nappy bag after he has been changed.

1 Jake stops what he is doing when he hears a noise of a plane passing overhead.

2 He looks up out of the window to confirm what he predicted is correct. He is, and says, 'Plane'.

1 Ophelia has found a recently bought toy and gives it to Melanie.

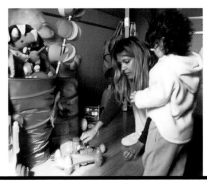

2 Melanie demonstrates how the toy works. She uses the hammer to bang one of the pegs...

3 ...which makes an unexpected squeaking noise. Melanie shows Ophelia her delight, 'Wow!'

4 Melanie turns the toy over and hammers the peg again to repeat the noise.

5 She then passes the hammer to Ophelia to try.

6 Ophelia settles down happily to copy her mother.

7 She turns the toy over and over again, hammering the coloured pegs to see what noise each one makes.

8 Ophelia is captivated by the toy and is quite happy to play while Melanie is sitting close by.

⁰⁰📷 *Picture story*

POSTING SHAPES

EMILY *15 months*

Emily needs her mother, Corinne, to help her with the 'post the bricks' shapes game. Emily demonstrates she has learned that the game is made up of different components that are all needed together, in order to play the game.

Emily also shows that she understands that when an object falls out of her sight it has not disappeared, but that it has fallen in a downwards direction and that she can predict successfully where it has landed. As she looks down, she shows no surprise to see it on the floor. Emily's understanding of how objects behave when they fall has been confirmed.

1 Corinne, Emily's mother, is showing her some coloured bricks.

5 Emily had seen it on a shelf.

9 Corinne swops the bricks round...

10 ... giving Emily the chance to successfully post the square brick, which she does.

11 Next the trianglar brick ...

2 Emily looks up, raising her hand in a circular motion, brushing Corinne's face.

3 As she nears the top of the circular motion, she points her finger and vocalises.

4 Corinne looks at where Emily is pointing. Emily makes her intentions clear, showing Corinne she needs the wooden frame to enable the 'post the bricks' shape game to start.

6 Corinne gets the frame and the game begins. Emily successfully pushes the round brick through the round slot.

7 Emily finds the square and triangle shapes more difficult to post. Corinne holds the frame while Emily tries.

8 Emily outstretches her arms, her palms facing upwards indicating to her mother she needs help.

12 ....and success, the game is complete.

13 Emily repeats the game, but the yellow triangular brick has slipped from the frame.

14 Emily is looking in the direction of the floor where the brick has fallen.

continues overleaf...

📽 *Picture story*

POSTING SHAPES

continued from previous page

EMILY 15 months

15 She points to the fallen brick and vocalises to Corinne.

EMIL 20 months

Emil is older than Emily. He is not only able to choose the game he wants to play, but he also knows where to find it; he can play with it on his own, and this time return it to where he found it.

Emil is showing that he is starting to put order in his life and to make sense of his world.

1 Emil has chosen the 'post the bricks' shapes game from the toy cupboard and has settled down to play.

4 But he has learned a different way to solve the problem. He takes the lid off!

16 Corinne reaches and picks it up.

17 The game commences again.

18 But Emily becomes tired with the game. She pushes the frame away with her feet, showing Corinne that she has had enough.

2 He has no problems in posting the round shape.

3 He is not so sure about the square shape...

5 Emil has now finished the game and starts to pick up the toy, returning it to the cupboard.

⚈ *Picture story*

FIRST STEPS TOWARDS PRETEND PLAY

The power of imagination

Children who can pretend can begin to represent the world in an imaginary way in their own minds.

To be able to 'pretend play', children need the ability to remember images. With the help of words and pictures they can begin to hold the images they see in their minds and recall them when needed. This is the beginning of thinking and of being able to follow a situation in the real world through their imagination.

EMILY *15 months*

Emily shows us that she is able to pretend there is tea in the cup.

1 Emily has picked out a cup from her toy basket.

4 Even though she finds there is no liquid in the cup, Emily's tongue comes out…

5 …and she pretends to drink liquid from the cup.

6 She tilts her head right back, before…

2 She offers it to her mother, Corinne, who says, *'Emily have some tea'*.

3 Emily puts her hand in the cup to feel if there is liquid in it.

7 …showing us she can even manage to imagine how lovely it tastes!

DEFINITION BY USE

During their second year, children start to use toys in a representative way, associating the toys they play with to the world they live in.

Cars are pushed along the floor, toy animals cuddled and dolls begin to be treated as separate beings which need to be fed, dressed and given instructions.

This shows a child can put together different toys in a meaningful way.

EMILY *15 months* shows her mother, Corinne, she has learned that a toy car is pushed along the floor.

📽 *Picture story*

TOM *20 months*

Tom puts three separate toys together in a meaningful way to make a coherent true-to-life story. He also shows he can imagine in his mind what the doll is experiencing when he gives her a bottle of milk.

1 Tom sees the doll on the floor and starts to pick it up …

2 … he places the doll in the carrier.

3 Tom now feeds the doll with a bottle. As he feeds, Tom shapes his mouth and makes sucking sounds, as if he is imaging what it is like for the doll to drink the milk.

TOM *19 months* takes great delight in pushing his toy fire engine along the floor; he also adds the various noises he associates with the vehicle.

TOM *20 months* cuddles his soft toy dog. He shows that he knows how to be gentle, caring and loving towards an animal.

4 He then places the bottle in the carrier…

5 …brings the straps together…

6 …and carries the doll away.

📽 *Picture story*

THE BEGINNINGS OF SHARING AN IMAGINARY WORLD WITH OTHER CHILDREN

Children can learn not only from their parents but also from other children

As children's imaginations grow, so the complexity of pretend play increases. They need less support from objects or props and in time the objects themselves will go. The magic of imagination has endless possibilities.

Eventually children become able to step into each other's worlds, visualise another's pretend play, and join in. (*See also 'Learning through play', page 284.*)

OPHELIA *20 months,*
JADE *8 years,* sister, HANNAH *8 years*

Ophelia is playing with sister, Jade, and Jade's friend, Hannah. Ophelia can now share her toys in an imaginary game with other children. She shows that she has learned the beginnings of pretend play by being able to imagine there is something tasty to eat from her bowl.

Ophelia knows what objects represent and their function. As she feeds and cuddles the doll, she is able to bring several events together and put them in order. Ophelia shows she can lose the support of one object (food in the bowl), by holding the image in her mind...

Text continues overleaf

3 Jade suggests the baby maybe hungry.

6 ...and puts the spoon to the doll's lips.

7 Ophelia then hands the bowl back...

1 Ophelia starts the game with Jade and Hannah. She gives Hannah a bowl and spoon.

2 Ophelia and Hannah watch Jade as she tastes the pretend food and finds it delicious.

4 Ophelia vocalises that she will feed the doll.

5 She takes the bowl...

8 ...and hugs the doll.

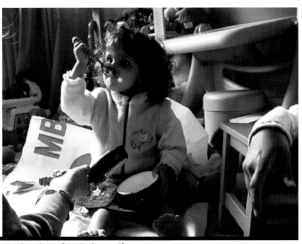

9 She then feeds herself...

continues overleaf...

📽 *Picture story*

THE BEGINNINGS OF SHARING AN IMAGINARY WORLD WITH OTHER CHILDREN

continued from previous page

...but Ophelia is puzzled by Jade and Hannah's attempt to include her in their total pretend play (without the use of any props).

10 ...and shares it with Hannah.

13 ...but looks intently at Jade's empty hand. Ophelia is puzzled as she cannot visualise what her sister is saying to her.

16 Hannah and Jade share their pretence together. Ophelia appears to be finding it difficult ...

11 Jade pretends to pour some tea from an imaginary tea pot into some cups for them all. Hannah watches, ready to join in.

12 As Jade hands a cup and saucer with the tea in it to Ophelia she says, 'Here's your cup of tea'. Ophelia goes to take it…

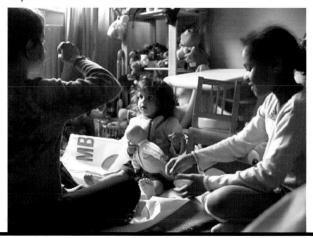

14 Ophelia looks at Hannah, who is pretending to drink her cup of tea…

15 …then back at Jade, who is doing the same.

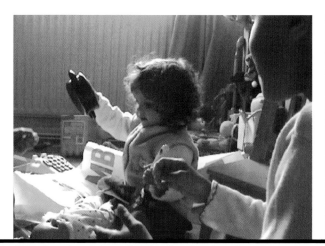

17 …but she picks up her familiar bowl and spoon …

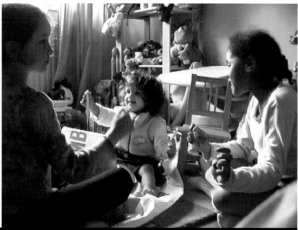

18 …and smiling, offers it to Hannah. By reintroducing the props into the game, Ophelia shows the older girls she can now join in the game again.

COPYING HOUSEHOLD CHORES

Children have watched their parents' activities since they were born, especially those of their prime carer. Although we adults may view household chores as boring and something to be done as quickly as possible, children are fascinated by what we are doing and often want to join in.

Observing and copying the day-to-day activities of parents helps children to make sense of the world they live in, and to feel part of that world by experiencing it at first hand. This helps children's creative imagination, which they can then apply in imaginary play; like an actor learning a part, the first step is to learn the words and actions, then rehearse, maybe improvise by adding an individual twist, and finally to perform.

EMIL *20 months* loves sweeping the slippery floor.

TOM *19 months*

At the moment, Tom loves to help his mother, Mandy, with the washing.

As Tom pulls the washing out of the machine and then puts it back, he is refining his understanding of the concept of in and out, and of open and shut.

1 Mandy asks Tom if he'd like to help take the washing out of the machine. He opens the washing machine door…

2 …and begins to pull out clothes and put them in the laundry basket.

6 Mandy encourages Tom to put it in the basket.

7 Tom decides he will also get in the basket.

8 Sitting down, he starts to put the washing back in the machine.

🎥 *Picture story*

OPHELIA *18 months*

1 Ophelia's mother, Melanie, is hoovering.

2 The noise is a familiar sound associated with an activity, and Ophelia wants to help. Melanie shortens the stem of the hoover to make it easier for Ophelia to use.

3 Although Ophelia may not really understand what a hoover does, she knows it is pushed backwards and forwards.

3 It takes a great effort for Tom to pull another article out.

4 When he succeeds he studies it…

5 …and triumphantly shows Mandy.

9 Tom soon finds opening and shutting the door of the machine more fun. Mandy feels it is time to end the game and distracts Tom by asking him to put some rubbish in the bin.

10 He eagerly takes the rubbish…

11 …and puts it in the bin.

COPYING EVERYDAY LIFE

Parents may not consider some of their children's attempts to copy day-to-day activities very helpful: posting objects into the video, pouring all the bubblebath into the bath, cleaning the floor with a tea-towel, or using a hair brush to clean the toilet, for example. Much of children's play may appear to be without method or even deliberately destructive, but it is not. They are trying to discover how things work, and make meaning of an activity by copying adult behaviour.

📽 *Picture story*

OPHELIA 18 months

Ophelia loves music and her sister Jade often lets Ophelia use her CD player. Jade is at school today and Ophelia is trying to play some music herself. She knows some of the sequence of actions she must do but not the order in which they have to be carried out, and she misses out the most important step – to open the CD player.

Ophelia has no concept that a CD or the player can be broken or damaged, she is simply copying the actions of her sister that she has observed.

> ### NOTE
> *To avoid unwanted help around the house, move objects out of the way or place them out of the child's reach.*

MONA 16 months likes to hold her parents' phone. She presses the buttons, but does not understand dialling, or that she may be calling someone.

TOM 19 months

Tom has found some typed papers lying around the house and has taken them very purposefully to the sofa; making sure he is sitting comfortably, he pretends to 'read' them.

He shows that he understands that the marks on the pages represent words and that words are read and spoken, but he has no idea of their meaning or of the papers' possible value to their owner. Tom is copying his father, Dave.

1 Tom laughs as his mother Mandy asks, 'What are you doing?'

1 Ophelia finds the CD player and looks up to see if there is a response.

2 She puts on the head phones, but they slip off as they are set up for Jade's head size.

3 Then she pushes the CD on to the top of the player.

4 Removing the CD, Ophelia pushes the play button.

2 He 'reads' the papers and babbles away to himself.

3 Tom turns the typed papers over and over until he eventually gets bored and discards them.

‼ *Picture story*

COPYING MUMMY'S AND DADDY'S PERSONAL ACTIVITIES

Children watch their parents not only completing day-to-day tasks around the house, but also their personal activities, such as washing, dressing, shaving and putting on make-up. Some of these are fascinating and children want to copy them.

In our modern western society parents may be concerned if their young boy wants to dress up in his mother's clothes, put on make-up or want ribbons in his hair, but we think nothing of a girl wearing trousers. There are many cultures around the world who dress differently from our own, where a boy wearing a skirt or putting colour on his face is deemed perfectly normal, yet a girl wearing trousers may be frowned upon.

Children of this age have no sense of what gender they are or what it means. It is therefore perfectly acceptable for boys and girls to experience what each parent does as this gives the child an opportunity for the development of flexible thinking and a better understanding of social roles in their world.

JAKE *24 months*

Jake loves to join in when his mother, Sarah, puts on her make-up in the morning.

4 Sarah has just finished with the blusher brush and Jake indicates that he wants to use it now.

HANNAH *19 months*

Hannah's father, Clive, sometimes has a shave when she is in the bath. Hannah likes to join in and help with the activity.

1 Clive puts some shaving foam onto Hannah's hand.

2 She begins to rub some foam on Clive's chin...

1 Jake jumps on to the bed to join Sarah who has started to get her make-up out.

2 He holds up a small container and asks what it is. Sarah explains to him that *'You put it on your eyes'*.

3 Jake does exactly as Sarah has said and puts the container on his eyes.

5 Just as his mother has done, Jake carefully brushes his cheek whilst looking in the mirror.

6 Jake then sees Sarah applying make-up to her eyes, and copies his mother, using the blusher brush.

7 He gives the brush back to Sarah, and the activity is complete.

3 ...before rubbing some foam onto her own chin...

4 ...followed by Clive's chin...

5 ...and finally his nose!

Picture story

SPATIAL AWARENESS (1)

Spatial awareness: *understanding of where things are in relation to other things*

At this age, children can start to relate small toys to real objects, but as yet they cannot relate the scale of different toy objects to each other, and cannot understand why sometimes a toy falls out (if it is too small) or will not go in (if it is too large).

EMILY *15 months*

Emily walks into her sister Megan's room, and finds a toy buggy. Emily attempts to put a miniature pet dog in the buggy and push it around, but the dog keeps falling out. Megan is unusually tolerant as she patiently watches as her sister unknowingly destroys the game she had been playing.

4 ...and places the buggy on the floor. Emily puts a tiny dog in the buggy and rocks it back and forth.

TOM *19 months*

Tom plays with his garage. He refines his understanding of in and out, push and pull, looking around and through.

1 As Tom looks through his garage, he sees a bear. He puts his hand through the garage and attempts to grasp it.

2 Tom peers over the top of the garage to visually locate the bear.

3 He successfully pulls the bear through the garage...

1 Megan is playing with her dolls' house toys and has them carefully arranged on the floor. Megan greets her sister as she enters the room.

2 Emily vocalises to Megan as she squats down.

3 Emily picks up a buggy...

5 The dog is too small and slips out of the buggy. Emily retrieves it.

6 As their mother, Corinne, passes. Emily tries once more to put the dog in the buggy...

7 ...and again tries to rock the buggy.

4 ...and pushes it back out.

5 He then pushes a much smaller toy through the garage.

6 But this time, rather than pull the toy, Tom chooses to walk round the garage to grasp it, even though it is a smaller toy than the bear.

📽 *Picture story*

SPATIAL AWARENESS (2)

Children will use experience to find out something about the world around them at every opportunity. They often repeat actions which to many adults may seem 'mindless'. It is anything but.

Children, like scientists, don't give up if they come across an exception to the rule; they learn from it and discover more about how that object behaves, the property of it and, what happens to it if...?

EMILY *15 months*

Emily seems to be interested in the fact that her head touches the tray and the feeling of the solid object on her head. She bobs up and down and tries to peer over the top of the tray as if assessing the height of the tray in relation to her own height.

4 ...and down again, each time touching her head on the underside of the tray.

5 She steps back, looks at and touches the tray.

OPHELIA *18 months*

Ophelia is finding out about distance as she chooses to put her toys back in the container.

1 Without looking, Ophelia uses her outstretched hand to see if she can put a toy back in the container.

2 She is successful, but needs to check that the toy did in fact go in.

1 By chance, Emily's head touches the top of her highchair tray.

2 She ducks down…

3 …and back up again…

6 Still with her hand holding the tray, she pushes her head underneath.

7 Emily then touches the tray with two hands and lifts herself up on tip toes…

8 …to try and see above it.

3 Ophelia repeats the action a little further away from the container, but she finds it more difficult to put the next toy in …

4 …the toy just slips out. She reaches to get it…

5 …and this time looks as she puts the toy in the container.

🎥 *Picture story*
SPATIAL AWARENESS (3)

OPHELIA *18 months*

As Ophelia plays, she discovers that she can hit something and make a sound without looking at it. She is confirming her understanding of cause and effect, space and distance.

1 As Ophelia swings a pop-out 'puppet on a stick' over her shoulder, she makes contact with a ball in the toy basket.

4 Surprised, she looks down to see what made the sound...

7 ...then down to the toy for the sound.

8 The repetitive action gets the attention of her mother, Melanie, who asks for the 'puppet on a stick'...

2 When she swishes the 'puppet on a stick' down again...

3 ...she hits a toy on the floor, which makes a sound.

5 ...and hits it again to make sure.

6 Without needing to look, Ophelia swings the 'puppet on a stick' and makes contact with the ball in the toy basket again ...

9 ...Ophelia turns and once again hits the ball...

10 ...before giving the puppet to Melanie, who distracts Ophelia by explaining how the 'puppet on a stick' can be played with.

📽 *Picture story*

EXPERIMENTING (1)

Children can play with the simplest of every-day objects and learn from them.

EMILY *15 months*

1 Emily puts the pasta in the mortar.

JAKE *24 months* helps wash up. As he plays in the sink he learns about pouring from one beaker to another.

TOM *19 months*

1 Tom has found a tea-towel.

5 ...until he lets it sink to the floor.

Emily is playing happily in the kitchen with a pestle and mortar, a metal jug, and some dried pasta. Corinne takes advantage of Emily's interest in experimenting to get on with preparing tea.

2 She grinds it with the pestle, listening to the sound...

3 ...and pours pieces of pasta into the metal container.

Tom plays with a tea-towel.

2 As he spins the tea-towel around, it flies out beside him.

3 Tom turns and turns as he watches the tea-towel fly through the air...

4 ...making different shapes...

6 Tom drags the tea-towel as he slides it along behind him and walks into the living room where...

7 ...he uses the tea-towel in a more familiar way to wipe the TV remote...

8 ...before he puts them both down and ends the game, as a favourite toy takes his attention.

EXPERIMENTING (2)

As mentioned earlier (*see 'Posting shapes', page 168*), children have learned about gravity. They know that if they drop an object it will fall to the ground and have been repeatedly testing this theory with different objects (including food) for some time.

They are also learning other laws of physics: how objects behave in differing properties – water and air; discovering if objects in water float before sinking, or just float or just sink; watching balloons and bubbles float in air before sinking to the ground or floating up in a breeze before disappearing altogether.

Learning these new laws also involves children in continual repetition to enable them to grasp and eventually predict what an object will do in a particular set of circumstances.

🎥 *Picture story*

HANNAH *12 months*

1 Hannah takes a dry flannel and watches as she drags it over the surface of the water.

1 OPHELIA *18 months* tries to push a ball under the water in her bath…

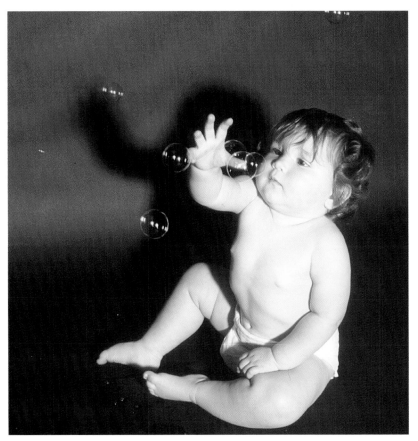

HANNAH *16 months* is absorbed in trying to touch a bubble without it bursting and disappearing.

During Hannah's bath-time she loves to play with a flannel before trying to wash herself.

2 She then scrunches up the flannel...

3 ...and puts her hands on her legs as she waits, looks, focusing all her attention on the flannel, to see what will happen.

4 As the flannel unravels and begins to sink, Hannah very carefully touches it.

2 ...to Ophelia's surprise and delight it pops up and floats beside her.

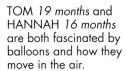

TOM *19 months* and HANNAH *16 months* are both fascinated by balloons and how they move in the air.

🎥 *Picture story*

TIDY-UP TIME

Children of this age do not yet understand the true concept of 'tidying up'. The apparent randomness of their disorder is their way of trying to understand the workings of objects that surround them. They naturally love to take things out from one place, look at them and put them back somewhere else – maybe not always where adults would like. This repeated sorting helps children categorise objects and refine the concept of in and out, which in time will help them to become organised and to create order in their environment.

OPHELIA *18 months*

Ophelia spends a lot of time in her room emptying her toy containers on to the floor and sorting through her toys.

OPHELIA *18 months*

Ophelia also enjoys putting the toys back in the toy container.

1 Ophelia is putting the toy container in position.

2 She decides to pick up a toy...

TOM *19 months*

Tom and his mother, Mandy, have just finished looking at two books together.

1 Mandy asks Tom to put the books away.

2 The books live in the toy chest. This time Tom decides to put one book away, on top of the toy chest.

1 Although the toy container is quite large for her…

2 …Ophelia manages to turn it upside down.

3 With all the toys now visible on the floor, she can choose the ones she wants.

3 …and puts it in the container.

4 Ophelia looks to her mother, Melanie, who praises her to give her encouragement.

5 Ophelia happily continues to put the toys away.

3 The book slides down the top of the chest and Tom laughs as he looks to Mandy to check her reponse. Mandy smiles and praises him for his success in putting the book away.

4 Tom is about to repeat the action with the second book. He holds on to it …

5 …and this time tries to see where it goes.

🎥 *Picture story*

OPHELIA *18 months*

LITTLE EXPLORERS – INTO EVERYTHING (1)

Beware, cupboards can be dangerous

Children love to open and shut doors, gates, drawers and cupboards. They are refining the concepts of open–shut and push–pull. By testing and experiencing the mechanics of these different actions they learn the workings of them and the many variations that are available in different circumstances.

Children's interest also cannot stop at the opening and shutting of a door, because within, there is usually (in the child's eye) a treasure-chest of goodies waiting to be investigated. The need for children to learn about everything they come across makes cupboards an exciting place to explore, but they do not understand the potential danger.

1 Ophelia has opened the cupboard under the sink and discovered an interesting box.

5 Ophelia finds there is a slimy liquid on one of the pots which gets on her finger.

SAFETY NOTE

A great many potentially dangerous household items are stored in kitchen cupboards. Safety catches on doors can help prevent accidents. For safety's sake make sure young children are not left unsupervised when in the kitchen or other places where they may have access to cleaning or other harmful materials.

9 Once again, she takes the 'bibic' out of the box.

*Ophelia shows the attraction and potential danger
that can be found in a kitchen cupboard.*

2 In the box is a shiny packet. She says, 'bibic' (biscuit).

3 Ophelia returns the packet of soap to the box.

4 She gets more things out of the cupboard to look at.

6 She examines her finger.

7 Ophelia goes to put the box back in the cupboard...

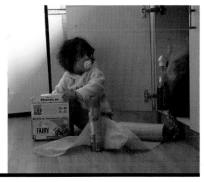

8 ...but decides against it.

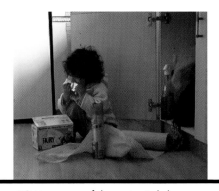

10 Unaware of the potential danger to herself, Ophelia bites it...

11 ...but it seems unfamiliar...

12 ...and she returns it once again to the box.

continues overleaf...

📽 *Picture story*

LITTLE EXPLORERS – INTO EVERYTHING (1)

continued from previous page

OPHELIA *18 months*

13 Ophelia looks up to see her mother, Melanie, enter the kitchen, and smiles. By smiling, Ophelia shows that she does not yet understand if her actions are right or wrong, she just knows there are some things she cannot do. She will learn from Melanie's response.

17 ...and puts it to her mouth...

21 However, when Ophelia is told, '*No, it's not a "bibic",*' she grabs it out of the box, and runs away.

14 Melanie says, *'Ophelia, what are you doing in the cupboard?'* Ophelia, still smiling, shows Melanie exactly what she has been doing. She opens the box...

15 ...and vocalises to her mother as she shuts the box.

16 Ophelia then takes the 'bibic' out of the box...

18 ...before returning it to the box.

19 Ophelia invites her mother to join her.

20 Melanie helps Ophelia return everything to the cupboard.

22 Melanie follows, and says *'Ophelia...'* to make it clear that she wants the soap back. Ophelia throws the 'bibic'...

23 ...and then herself on the floor. Melanie's consistent response shows Ophelia that she cannot take an object from the cupboard.

🎥 *Picture story*

LITTLE EXPLORERS – INTO EVERYTHING (2)

A safe kitchen cupboard

EMILY *15 months*

Emily is in the kitchen with her mother, Corinne, who is cooking the family evening meal. Emily likes to be with her mother in the kitchen but quickly becomes bored. Corinne has found ways in which they can be near one another, yet Emily can play while Corinne carries on with cooking. Emily is too young to help Corinne with the cooking but she can safely copy some of the activities involved on the floor.

To enable this, Corinne has made one of the kitchen cupboards safe for Emily to explore.

1 Emily waits patiently as Corinne prepares some items for Emily.

4 ...uses the pestle to crunch the pasta...

7 Corinne keeps a check on how Emily is doing.

2 She places them on the floor.

3 Emily looks in the mortar and…

5 …then pours the pieces into the jug…

6 …and back into the mortar.

8 Emily puts her thumb in her mouth for comfort. She has finished the game and…

9 …discovers that by standing on the mortar…

continues overleaf…

Picture story
LITTLE EXPLORERS –
INTO EVERYTHING (2)
continued from previous page

EMILY *15 months*

10 …she can see into her familiar kitchen cupboard.

13 Emily decides to open her cupboard…

14 …and get some more containers…

15

16 …which she brings out…

11 Corinne comes to assist Emily in getting some small bowls…

12 …and helps tidy up the pasta with Emily.

17 …and continues to play happily, allowing Corinne to continue cooking.

PLAYING WITH OTHER CHILDREN (1)

Parallel play

📽 *Picture story*

Children are both fascinated and intrigued by other children, especially those around the same size as themselves, and they are eager to come into contact. However, toys are just as interesting, and children often play with toys alongside one another, but independently; this is known as parallel play. During parallel play, children will be very aware of what the other is doing and watch each other. With limited language skills, imitating each other's actions is the main form of communication, but as this is the beginning of building relationships with their peers, they will need some support from their parents.

Children of this age remain 'self-centred'. They are beginning to learn the concept of others having a 'self' of their own, but they may still assume that everything they see is theirs. Not having the skill to read another's mind makes it impossible for children to empathise – to be able to put themselves into someone else's place and imagine what a situation is like from another's perspective. Everyone else's world is their world, nothing else exists. This makes the concept of sharing difficult for children to comprehend.

When interacting with others, a child begins to learn about empathy by experiencing what it feels like when another child won't share. Until children develop a sense of self they cannot realise someone else feels pain if they are not experiencing it themselves; so if a child plays with another and it all goes wrong, and one child's frustration is vented by being aggressive to the other (for example, biting or scratching), the outburst can be frightening for both children. The perpetrator will not understand why he or she has done something wrong, let alone be able to be sorry, or know what 'sorry' means.

Repeated and sensitive guidance from adults can help a child understand that others have needs and feelings as well themselves, and in time 'sorry' will become meaningful and sincere, along with physical acts of sympathy towards others who are hurt or upset. So, although children still play alongside each other, rather than with each other, they are beginning to look at what the other is doing and learning to interact with them.
(See 'Empathy', page 282.)

1 Emil has picked up a toy belonging to Sasha, to play with.

5 ...as she grabs the toy...

7 Emil lets go, looking to his mother for support.

EMIL *20 months,*
SASHA *17 months*

When Sasha visits her grandmother, who lives next door to Emil, they often play together.

2 Sasha has seen Emil with the toy.

3 Sasha's eyes are fixed on the toy as she immediately walks towards Emil.

4 She makes no eye contact with Emil...

6 ...and pulls it towards her.

EMIL *20 months* and SASHA *17 months* 'play together'.

8 Sasha returns the toy to her grandmother. Emil finds another toy with which to play.

📽 *Picture story*

PLAYING WITH OTHER CHILDREN (2)

SAPPHIRE *14 months* and
HUGO *14 months (twins)*,
EMILY *15 months*

Sapphire and Hugo have come round to play with Emily. Although they have met several times before, they have not seen each other for about 6 months.

When the toy basket is brought out, Emily finds it difficult to share her toys with the twins. All three will believe everything they see is theirs and they have no concept of sharing. Whilst Emily's mother, Corinne, and the twins' mother, Zoë, chat together, the three children are left to try and organise for themselves which toys they will play with.

Hugo is walking independently, but his twin, Sapphire, is still at the cruising stage. Her inability to walk means she has to remain at her mother's side, but she is clearly as interested in the toys as Emily and Hugo.

1 Emily has chosen a ball and Hugo a musical box. Sapphire looks on.

4 Emily immediately picks up the ball again.

7 Hugo attempts a smile.

8 Hugo is calm as Emily approaches and takes the musical box from him.

2 Emily points and vocalises to Hugo that she wants the musical box.

3 Sapphire gets her mother's attention as she needs help. Emily puts the ball down, intent on getting the box from Hugo; but he now places his hand on the ball.

5 Zoë helps Sapphire while her brother holds on to the box, his eyes remaining fixed on the ball.

6 Emily holds the ball close to herself as Hugo lifts the box. Sapphire watches Emily intently.

9 She steps aside and holds the box as far away as she can. Hugo is unsure.

10 Both Hugo and Emily look to Zoë for her response. She returns his look but says nothing.

continues overleaf...

11 Hugo dives for the toy basket again and this time grabs a cube. Although Emily has moved away, Sapphire is watching her.

12 Emily sees Hugo with the cube and moves towards him.

15 In a matter of seconds, Hugo has grabbed the ball and Emily the cube.

16 As Emily turns to walk away, she manages to hook the ball back from Hugo and successfully acquires both toys.

19 Sapphire gestures her need again. Zoë looks towards the basket for another toy.

20 Zoë introduces a new toy which Emily now wants. Hugo's eyes are still on the cube. Corinne gets more toys out of the basket.

13 Hugo clutches the cube close to him. Emily vocalises that she wants the cube.

14 Corinne intervenes and takes the muscical box from Emily and switches it on for everyone to hear. Emily drops the ball, but still looks intently at Hugo, who has the cube.

17 Hugo grabs the ball. Emily turns back as the ball is taken and Sapphire joins in, vocalising and gesturing that she wants the cube. Zoë and Corinne now look on.

18 Hugo is determined to hang on to the ball as Emily makes a grab for it. Sapphire joins in. Corinne and Zoë prepare to assist.

21 Emily drops the cube, Zoë takes the ball, and Hugo spots another toy on the floor.

22 Sapphire is now on the sofa with a toy that has caught her interest. Emily and Hugo are now occupied with different toys. The ball and cube do not now seem to be so important.

SPONTANEOUS GAMES (1)

Spontaneous games and play can happen anywhere, at any time and without the use of sophicated props. The freedom this type of unpredicted play offers makes the games exciting, with a high thrill factor.

Everyone interprets spontaneous games differently, and children can learn from this. Games with older siblings, their friends and adults other than their parents helps develop social interaction and the ability to build trust towards others (*see also* 'Rhyme, Rhythm and Song', page 150).

📽 *Picture story*

JAKE *24 months*
Jake and his mother, Sarah, play 'Hide-and-seek'.

Mona's sister, Khadja, makes it quite clear in her approach to MONA *16 months* that she is prepared for some spontaneous play.

OLIVIA *20 months*

1 As Olivia and Helen sit together on the sofa, Helen spots Olivia's toes. She gently wiggles her big toe.

2 Then Olivia points to her other toe...

3 ...and Helen wiggles that one, too. A simple game begins.

1 Sarah is getting the chalk board ready for an activity.

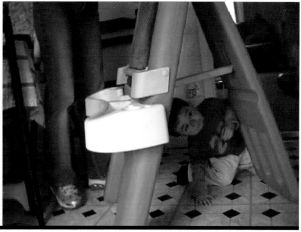

2 Jake is looking underneath to check the board is fixed.

3 He hears Sarah call out, *'Where's Jake?'* He remains very still, taking the cue that a game is about to start.

4 Jake screams out as his mother peeps round the board and asks again.

5 Jake turns around as Sarah smiles and says, *'There you are ...'*

6 *'...I'm going to get you!'* she says. Jake squeals with delight.

📷 *Picture story*

SPONTANEOUS GAMES (2)

'Peek-a-boo'

Older children are less predictable with their play, often not explaining what is going to happen beforehand, leaving the younger child to work it out for themselves in order to be able to join in.

OPHELIA *20 months,*
JADE *8 years, sister,*
HANNAH *8 years*

1 Hannah and Jade decide to play a 'Peek-a-boo' game with Ophelia and they cover their eyes. Ophelia looks at them.

2 They both suddenly uncover their eyes and say, 'Peek-a-boo'.

3 As Jade repeats the action, Ophelia has already copied the girls by covering her eyes...

4 ...and uncovers them saying, 'Boo'.

5 Now Hannah and Jade follow Ophelia's lead and they all cover their eyes at the same time...

OPHELIA *20 months,*
JADE *8 years, sister,*
HANNAH *8 years*

'Hide-and-seek'

Older children are also able to help a younger child learn how a game is played. Here, Ophelia's sister, Jade, and her friend, Hannah, pretend to look for and find Ophelia.

1 Jade and Hannah have hidden from Ophelia behind a curtain. Ophelia has run to find them.

2 They decide to play hide-and-seek and that it is Ophelia's turn to hide. She is persuaded to go behind the curtain.

6 ...ready for the synchronised loud, '*Boo*'!

3 After counting, Hannah comes out from a bedroom and says, '*I wonder if Ophelia is under the radiator!*'

4 Jade follows and says, '*Is she under the table... no!*'

5 Then they both find Ophelia behind the curtain and tickle her!

FOOD

Some parents worry that their children are not eating enough food or getting the right nutrition, and go to great lengths to try and persuade their child to eat more. Young children will not starve themselves, and forcing them to eat may lead to eating problems in the future. Provided children are healthy, bright-eyed, and full of energy and life, there is no need for concern. If complete meals are rejected by a child, parents can help ensure he or she gets sufficient nutrition by providing a selection of finger foods. Children of this age are refining the ability to pick up small objects with their thumb and index finger (pincer grasp), and small or chopped-up foods such as peas, raisins, fruit and vegetables, cheese and cold meats will hold their interest during meal-times and help to establish a routine.

Some children may go through phases of only wanting to eat the same food, and then switch to another. Their body will be telling them what they need, and it is unlikely this phase will last for a long while, or become permanent.

Children of this age are learning about the laws of physics: cause and effect, in and out, up and down, and gravity. Mealtimes and food provide the opportunity for children to continue to explore, dissect, sort and learn about the properties different foods have to offer. Dropping food on the floor and looking to see where it has gone (gravity), or chewing up food and spitting it out to see what they have done to it (cause and effect) are just two activities that are quite normal, but which can cause conflict. By preparing before-hand, such as using a plastic mat to cover the floor, children can have the freedom they need to experiment. Spoons, cup, and bowls also provide valuable experimental play as they practise how to use them.

Parents may feel it is their responsibility to spoonfeed children and not let them take charge for themselves. However, children need to feel in control and mealtimes can easily turn into a food game (*see 'Sarah's story: Lunch time', page 70*), as parents 'battle' with their children to try and get

them to eat. This can develop into feeding problems such as children refusing to open their mouths, gagging or spitting food out. Children are very sensitive to the reactions of their parents, so it is better to use ignoring and distraction (*see page 58*).

By respecting children's own needs, reading their cues and being consistent, mealtimes will become an enjoyable, sociable event.

EATING TOGETHER

Mealtimes are a social event where members of the family can come together and share the events of the day, as well as the food that is offered. Children at day-care centres also enjoy the social aspects of being together and eating. Although children of this age are not able to contribute to the conversation, they learn a great deal from watching and listening, which helps develop social skills, as well as their sense of well-being.

🎥 *Picture story*

EMIL *20 months*

Emil's family always eat together. Even though Emil is not feeling hungry tonight, he still likes to take his place around the family meal table.

1 Emil climbs up to get into his high chair.

2 He is helped by his mother, Abi.

3 Abi offers him some food, but Emil raises his hand and...

4 ...pushes Abi's hand away, gesturing he does not want food now.

5 Emil gestures and vocalises his need to be with Abi.

6 Emil is calm now that he is sitting on Abi's lap. He watches closely as she uses her fork.

🎥 *Picture story*
DEVELOPING SKILLS THROUGH FOOD
Furthering dexterity and social skills

Food presents children with an ideal opportunity to develop new skills and to experiment. They frequently use it as a learning tool, with the added advantage that food can also be eaten!

Offering food to another helps children to develop social skills as well as reinforcing their emerging concept of sharing.

EMILY *15 months*
Emily enjoys a snack of raisins whilst practising a skill.

EMIL *20 months*, SASHA *17 months*
Emil and Sasha find sharing toys difficult at the moment, but they are learning about social skills by sharing food.

1 Emil's mother, Abi, has given him two rice cakes. She explains to Emil that one is for Sasha.

2 Emil walks towards Sasha with the two rice cakes.

1 Emily's mother, Corinne, puts some raisins on the step of the highchair.

2 Emily is practising using her pincer grip to pick up the individual raisins. Her left hand is tensely splayed out as all her concentration is focused on the task.

3 Despite the fact that she displaces some raisins, she successfully picks one up and pops it in her mouth.

4 Emily looks to her mother and shows the pleasure in her achievement.

3 Emil is successfully able to give the rice cake to Sasha. She is able to accept the one that Emil has offered.

4 They both eat the rice cakes.

☷ *Picture story*

LEARNING THROUGH FOOD

Food as play and a learning tool

By playing with food, children are learning a great deal about the various textures, tastes and properties of what they have been given to eat. Sometimes, though, food may be interesting for completely different reasons, and as adults tend to focus on the eating aspect of food, they may miss the other activities that are taking place.

EMILY *15 months*

Emily has been given half a plum and she has vocalised for the other half, which her mother, Corinne, gives to her. Emily is not interested in eating the plum at the moment, but shows how completely engrossed she is in the two halves of the plum.

Emily practises the skill of co-ordinating the movement of both hands as well as her spatial awareness. She moves her hands at the same time and mirrors her actions, as she skilfully places the two halves of the plum on different parts of her tray.

1 Emily's mother Corinne, gives Emily the other plum half.

5 She again takes her hands away and studies them.

9 ...and then at the half plum on her left.

10 Emily then picks up both plum halves...

11 ...and places them side by side on her right hand side.

2 Emily places her splayed hands on top of the upturned plum halves.

3 She takes her hands away and looks at the plum halves, which have not moved.

4 Emily then takes hold of the two plum halves and places them towards the far edge of her tray.

6 This time she decides to lift the plum halves up high and…

7 …quickly place them on the tray. Lifting her hands back in the air…

8 …she looks at the half plum on her right…

12 Emily takes her hands away and looks at the plum halves in their new positions.

13 Once again she picks them up, and this time places them on her left hand side. She takes her hands away… looks at the plum halves…

14 …and then looks up to Corinne for a response. Although Corinne is not entirely sure what Emily is trying to show her, she smiles and says, *'Clever girl.'*

📽 *Picture story*
FEEDING MYSELF
Showing I've had enough

Children take great delight in feeding themselves, even if the food does not always end up where it's supposed to!

Children learn eating skills by copying others and through trial and error. They also practise 'in and out' and 'sorting' when feeding themselves, and are able to show clearly when they have had enough to eat.

EMILY *15 months*
Emily has tea with her sister, Megan, and brother, Oliver.

1 Emily watches her mother, Corinne, as she blows the food to cool it down.

2 Emily takes a spoonful of food and copies her mother, blowing onto it.

6 Next, Emily uses her hand and fingers to scoop some food to her mouth.

7 Using both her fingers and the spoon, Emily takes food from the bowl and puts it onto the tray.

8 Some vegetables are then put into the bowl.

12 Corinne tries to encourage Emily to eat a little more; she first turns away, seeming to reject the food...

13 ...but then accepts and eats the spoonful Corinne offers her.

14 Corinne tries another spoonful. This time Emily's rejection is more pronounced; she retracts her head and pushes both the bowl and beaker away.

3 Emily's brother, Oliver, comes to the table and blows into her ear as he passes her. Emily turns her head away, showing that she does not want to play at the moment.

4 When Oliver has passed by, Emily watches him as she takes a drink from her beaker.

5 Emily changes her spoon to her right hand. She now begins to sort her food and starts by spooning some onto her tray.

9 Emily's concentration is broken momentarily as she enjoys watching Megan and Oliver who are sharing a joke.

10 Emily continues to look at them as she successfully scoops food into her mouth with her spoon.

11 Emily has now placed the beaker into her bowl, showing that she has finished.

15 As Corinne nears Emily's mouth she flings her head backwards and tightly shuts her mouth.

16 To make her intentions even clearer, Emily turns her head away and verbally protests, 'Urgh!'

17 Corinne takes the bowl and beaker away and leaves Emily, who contentedly surveys the food left on her tray.

📽 *Picture story*

FEEDING CAN BE MESSY BUT FUN!

Children watch how others use their hands or tools (eg knife, fork, spoon) to get different foods into their mouths, and then copy what they see. With practice, children develop skills and learn new techniques for eating as well as improving existing ones. It is a lengthy process, but one that should be encouraged, so that children do not learn to associate food and mealtimes with stress and anxiety.

SAPPHIRE and HUGO
14 months (twins)

1 Sapphire and Hugo are eating lunch. Zoë, their mother, is on hand to offer help if needed.

5 ...and tries sucking her fingers to get food into her mouth.

6 Her brother, Hugo, has mastered the use of a spoon and is able to use it get food into his mouth.

7 Sapphire now has a different spoon which she tries, using her other hand.

9 As Sapphire reaches out her hand, she squeezes the yoghurt through her fingers. Zoë puts some on her nose, which makes Hugo laughs.

10 Sapphire enjoys the moment and screws up her face as she turns away, smiling.

Sapphire and her brother Hugo have fun eating lunch. They enjoy the freedom of being able to experiment with food at the same time as feeding themselves.

2 Sapphire concentrates hard as she tries to get some food onto her spoon.

3 She lifts the spoon and turns it over as it nears her mouth. Her tongue comes out to coax the food into her mouth.

4 Although she is successful, Sapphire now puts her fingers into the bowl…

8

8 Next, it is time for pudding. Sapphire enjoys yoghurt, but she prefers to scoop it out of the pot with her whole hand, and then lick it from her palm.

BECOMING AWARE OF SELF: TOILET PRACTICE

Children have to be sufficiently self-aware before they can learn to use a toilet in preference to a nappy. This means they have to be at the right stage of physical and emotional development, and understand some sophisticated concepts before they can start. Children have been trying to make sense of 'their world' and put order into their lives for some time. Everything they have learned is through discovery, play, experimentation and exploration and children apply what they have learned in the past when confronted with something new. Simplistically, for the child, learning to use a toilet is just another task, but it is made all the more interesting by the fact that substances from their own body are involved, and it seems to be of great interest to their carers.

Parents and carers need to view the transition from nappy to toilet in the same context as other issues. Remember also that children have single-minded determination, they are easily distracted and have short memories; plus they are learning about cause and effect, how people react to the decisions they make, and 'what happens if...'.

Attempts to have children use a potty or toilet before they are receptive and developmentally ready, or to hurry the process, will not result in their being out of nappies any sooner, and may even slow the process down or cause conflict by drawing attention to negative behaviour. Being insensitive or having unrealistic expectations may

well undermine their developing sense of self. In time, children will become in complete control of where, when or even if he or she will go to the toilet.

The age at which a child will be developmentally ready to use a potty or toilet varies considerably, but it is unlikely to be much before the latter part of the second year, and when it happens, girls are generally quicker than boys.

Signs that a child is becoming aware are:
- Being able to physically sit still for a few minutes.
- Able to understand and follow two simple commands.
- Vocally coming out of the 'no' cycle.
- Being aware of their body parts.
- Starting to show an interest in, and imitating their parents' toilet activities.
- Knowing when they are wet, or 'dirty'.

When babies toilet, it is the result of a reflex action. This remains in place until around 18 months of age, when the reflex lessens and voluntary actions begin. At about the same time, children start to show more interest in their own bodies, exploring themselves, and especially their genitals. Children watch and observe the general day-to-day activites of those around them in order to learn, so it should not be a surprise when they

1 JAKE *24 months* has just had his nappy changed. He likes to hold the nappy bag and be involved in the activity.

2 Jake's mother, Sarah, asks him if he knows what to do with the nappy bag. He listens...

3 ...and goes straight to the bin where he successfully puts the nappy bag.

become interested in their parents' toilet activity, or their genitals. Adults should not be concerned as this is a first step towards becoming self-aware and using the toilet, and is almost always transitional. Children may also be fascinated with what we are doing in the toilet, which offers a good opportunity to talk about toileting. Some of their observations may be very direct or embarrassing, but any response should be calm, and if you feel unable to answer, find a distraction.

Some children show an interest in the toilet before their nerve paths are mature enough for them to know when they are wet, but listening and answering their questions helps to give them confidence. When children do become aware, their next step is to vocalise that they are wet and do not like it, or indicate this by trying to pull at their nappy. At this point you can encourage them towards a potty, or if preferred, to a child's toilet seat. Anything that comes out of their body is a part of them, and they are often very pleased with what they have produced. By letting the child flush the toilet and see what happens (cause and effect) we can support their need to have choices and feel they are in control.

A teddy or special doll can be be used as a teaching aid to encourage imitation and role-play games: 'Let's see if teddy wants to sit on the toilet. Can you show him how?' Sounds associated with the toilet can be a fun element, and so in time can aiming for boys to help their skill when standing up!

Journeys may be frustrating for parents, with lots of stops at short intervals, but children's urgency is real and immediate whilst they learn bladder control. Accidents may happen if a child is excited, laughing, or totally involved with an activity. If this happens, children can become upset or embarrassed, and may see it as a 'failure'. Learning to use the toilet requires a great deal of practice, and adults can support children by not making a fuss, and reminding them how much they have achieved so far: 'Do you remember when...'

HANNAH *2 years 6 months* has recently learned to use a toilet. Here she role-plays with her teddy, placing him on her child's seat, before carefully wiping his bottom. Hannah shows she can now relate her play to her own life.

Practising using the toilet should be an unpressured event, which takes as long as it takes for the individual child; it is not a race, and like any new acquired skill it is rewarding, another big achievement and a significant step towards independence.

NOTE: *During this time, children may appear to take a step back in their progress, reverting to more 'babylike' behaviour. This is perfectly normal.* (See 'Regression', page 101.)

CARA *3 years* can use the toilet on her own.

BECOMING AWARE OF SELF (1)

Children of this age are beginning to become aware that they are an individual and that they physically exist. They may know their reflection in a mirror but will still find it difficult to recognise themselves in photographs taken when they were younger, assuming it is another baby. This shows that children live very much in the present and have not yet developed an understanding of the past, or that they were once a baby.

Children of this age believe everyone exists in their present form, and that they do not change. They have yet to learn the concept of time and life; that babies grow to be children and then adults who in time become old. Children also assume that what they see, everyone else can too.

When OPHELIA *18 months*, looks at herself in the mirror she says, *'Ophelia'*, showing she recognises her own image.

OPHELIA *18 months*, has chosen a picture card of a mouse, and holds it up to show her mother, Melanie. The picture is facing towards Ophelia, but she assumes that because she can see the image, Melanie can also see that Ophelia has chosen the card with the mouse on.

JAKE *24 months*

1 Jake has put some bubbles on his chin and his mother, Sarah, shows him his reflection in a saucepan...

🎥 *Picture story*

OPHELIA *18 months*

Ophelia's mother, Melanie, has brought out the family photo album for them to look at.

1 Ophelia loves to look at the family photo album. She happily points out mummy and daddy to Melanie.

2 Melanie asks, 'Who's the baby?'

3 Ophelia appears not to be interested, and she turns the page. Melanie says, 'It's you, Ophelia.' Ophelia replies, 'Baby.'

OLIVIA *20 months*

Olivia and Helen are together watching a recent video of themselves.

1 Helen points to Olivia and asks, 'Who's that?'

2 Olivia points to herself and replies, 'Baby.' Helen says 'It's Olivia.'

Jake enjoys using lots of bubbles when he plays at washing up.

2 ...but the bubbles have already gone. Jake places his chin against his reflection.

3 Sarah suggests he gets some more bubbles to place on his chin. Jake takes some bubbles...

4 ...and rubs the bubbles, not on his own chin, but on the reflection of his chin in the saucepan.

📽 *Picture story*

BECOMING AWARE OF SELF (2)

Beginning to know my own body

As children become aware of self they begin to notice their own body parts and can put names to them.

1 Emily peers down and tries to locate her tummy button. Emily's mother, Corinne, waits to dress her.

EMILY *17 months*

When Emily is dressing she notices, and shows much interest in, her tummy button.

OPHELIA *18 months*

During games together, Ophelia's mother, Melanie, is starting to teach Ophelia the names to parts of her body.

1 Melanie touches her nose and says, 'Mummy's nose.'

JAKE *24 months*

Jake loves to point to, and say the name of different parts of his body. Jake is learning more each day.

1 Jake begins by touching his nose and saying, 'Nose.'

2 His mother, Sarah, joins in. Animatedly, they both say, 'Mouth…'

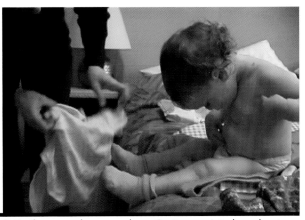

2 Corinne helps Emily by pointing to her new discovery saying, *'There it is, Emily's tummy button.'*

3 Emily peers down to where Corinne pointed, and puts her finger in to check. This is the first interest Emily has shown in her body.

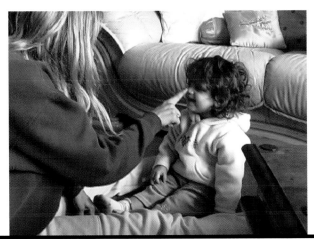

2 She then touches Ophelia's nose and says, *'Ophelia's nose.'*

3 They both touch their own noses. Ophelia is starting to learn the names of parts of her body.

3 *'...Tongue...'*

4 ...and a new one Jake learned yesterday, *'Elbow.'*

📽 *Picture story*

BEGINNINGS OF USING THE TOILET

Children begin to show signs of becoming ready to make the transition from wearing a nappy to using a toilet when they become interested in the toilet, and the activites that surround it. Wanting to help at nappy-change time, clutching at a nappy, and copying the activities of adults, are all signs a child is becoming aware.

This does not mean children will be able to use a toilet without a great deal of practice and patience. Children have short memories, and having completed part of the task, may become distracted and forget to complete the exercise. They may then want to come back soon afterwards to repeat it. Allowing them to do this, and become involved in ways such as pulling the chain and washing their hands after, helps to establish healthy routines and build confidence in their own ability to perform this new task.

OPHELIA *20 months*

Ophelia shows that she now knows she wants to go to the toilet by clutching at herself. Ophelia can also remove her nappy and put it in the bin. But when she is put on the toilet she jumps off, showing that whilst Ophelia is keen to mimic the actions, this time, she is not ready to use the toilet.

4 ...heads towards the bin.

JAKE *24 months*

Jake shows he is beginning to know the order of events involved in 'going to the toilet' as he is now happy to sit on the seat.

1 Jake is sitting on the toilet seat and his mother, Sarah, helps him to adjust his legs. Sarah reminds Jake to watch where he will 'go' while sitting.

2 Although Jake does not use the toilet, he reaches for the toilet paper...

3 ...and uses it to wipe himself.

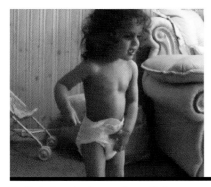

1 Ophelia clutches at herself showing she wants to go to the toilet.

2 She can easily remove her nappy…

3 …waving it triumphantly as she…

5 When her mother Melanie puts her on the toilet, Ophelia squirms to get down and protests.

6 When off the seat, however, she shows interest in the mechanics of the toilet seat and lifts it up.

7 Melanie asks her if she needs to go to the toilet and Ophelia turns and runs away.

4 Jake then decides he needs to push and shuts his eyes tightly as if making a great effort.

5 He gets off the toilet, and both he and Sarah peer into the bowl. Although Jake did not manage anything this time…

6 …he closes the seat lid and flushes the toilet. Jake shows that he knows, and will soon be able, to go to the toilet on his own.

SECTION FOUR

THE THIRD YEAR

PHYSICAL DEVELOPMENT

By the age of two, the progress children have made in their physical development brings a sense of confidence. As their coordination improves, they are better able to run – stopping and starting at will. This means obstacles can now be avoided. Other major achievements are walking up and down stairs, riding and steering a tricycle, and kicking a ball. However, those children who remain fearless are not yet aware of the danger in many of their activities.

ETHAN 2 *years 3 months*

1 Ethan bends his knees, and rests his hands on his thighs. Using all his concentration...

ETHAN 2 *years 3 months*

Ethan has yet to learn a sense of danger during certain activities.

1 Ethan climbs up the bookshelf in order to get himself a video.

2 Ethan's mother, Julie, quickly comes to hold him, and as she lifts him off...

3 ...says, 'No' to reinforce the danger of climbing the bookshelf. Julie then reminds Ethan that he can ask her for the video he wants.

Ethan is wearing his favourite T-shirt which has the motif of a frog on the front.

2 ...and the strength in his legs, he launches himself into the air...

3 ...and throws his legs and arms forward.

4 He lands by the chair in the same squatting position in which he started. Ethan shows his mother, Julie, he not only knows the movements of a frog, but he is now physically able to copy one. In his imagination he has become a leaping frog.

4 On another occasion, Ethan stands on a chair...

5 ...and uses it as a spring-board to launch himself though the air...

6 ...to where he lands safely on the sofa cushions.

FINE MOTOR SKILLS

Dexterity

Children now have much improved dexterity. Continually practising use of hand/eye co-ordination, and trial and error means
they have become capable of using many intricate fine movements to begin tasks such as dressing themselves. Children can
also feed themselves competently using a spoon, progressing to
a knife and fork (but will still sometimes regress to fingers), and
drink from an open cup without spilling. Other skills include
picking up large and small objects and placing them down accurately. They can make turning and screwing actions using their
fingers, thumbs and wrists.

FELIX *2 years 8 months* co-ordinates
both his hands enabling him to roll
out some dough.

JAYDEN *2 years 6 months* tries to
disentangle two plastic rings.

FELIX *2 years 8 months* uses hand/
eye co-ordination to drip glue from
his brush onto the box, whilst
carefully and accurately placing a
piece of paper on the top.

ETHAN *2 years 3 months* shows how
he is able to put a car key in a lock,
and then turn the key to open the
door.

PETER 2 *years 10 months*

*Peter is sufficiently competent
that he can complete a complex
task without having to look the
whole time.*

1 Peter is blowing some bubbles.

2 He decides he has finished and
puts the stick into the pot.

📽 *Picture story*

JAYDEN 2 *years 6 months*

Jayden decides to do some ironing, and combines different activities during his play.

1 Jayden has found the iron in the play kitchen. He takes it…

2 …over to the cooker, which he switches on by using his fingers and thumb in a turning action.

3 Jayden now irons the top of the cooker.

FELIX 2 *years 8 months*

Felix plays happily with the sand.

1 Felix fills up a bucket with sand.

2 He is able to turn it over and pull off the bucket, revealing a sand castle.

3 Peter uses his right hand and fingers to spin the top secure whilst firmly holding the bottle with his left hand.

4 To tighten the cap, Peter turns both hands in the opposite, and correct, direction.

5 Peter successfully completes the task.

EMOTIONAL DEVELOPMENT

📽 *Picture story*

USING EMOTIONS

No patience – can't wait. It has to be NOW!

Children have limited ability to be patient and wait for something. They are still learning the concept of time, and have limited understanding of past and future events; they live only in the present. Children may have learned the words, *'tomorrow'*, *'later'*, *'in a minute'* and *'wait there'*, but all they really understand is that they mean, *'not now'*. From past experience children have learned that 'wait a minute' produces no satisfactory result for them. Children are discovering that using their emotions can be an effective way to achieve what they want, and immediately.

ETHAN *2 years 3 months*

Ethan has recently come to understand that using his emotions and becoming upset is a good way to gain attention and achieve what he wants.

1 Ethan is listening to his brother, John's, music.

3 John asks Ethan, *'Shall I go and get it? You stay here.'*

6 Ethan cries out loudly as he points towards the staircase. He makes his intentions clear.

7 Ethan stops his protest as he gingerly starts to climb the stairs.

2 Ethan wants John to put his '*La La la*' music on.

4 As John moves to go upstairs and get the music for Ethan, Ethan protests that he wants to go too.

5 Ethan throws his head down and drops to the floor. He draws on all his emotional skills to show John how unhappy he is.

8 Halfway up, he turns and shouts in frustration, '*Stairs.*'

9 When Ethan reaches the top of the stairs he smiles, happy again.

📽 *Picture story*

CHOOSING

Showing personal preferences

Children begin to show preferences for toys, colours, playmates, how they wear their hair, as well as what they want to do. Showing likes and dislikes is an important way for them to express their individuality and feelings about themselves.

We may not always agree with children's choices (for example, when they pick different coloured socks to wear) but this can be avoided by offering the child a selection of clothes that will go together.

This all helps children learn about themselves and gain self-confidence as they move towards being independent and accepted by new friends outside the family. In time, comments made by their peers about their clothes will begin to become important.

ETHAN 2 *years 3 months*

Ethan likes to choose the clothes he wears. Ethan's mother, Julie, selects a few garments which she knows will go together.

1 Ethan's mother, Julie, knows he likes to choose which clothes he puts on in the morning.

4 Julie holds up both pairs of trousers and Ethan points to the red pair.

7 ...and then another. Ethan ignores the second T-shirt and confirm his wish to wear the former, by placing his hand on the first T-shirt, which is now on Julie's knee.

8 Julie puts the other clothes out of Ethan's sight, to avoid him changing his mind.

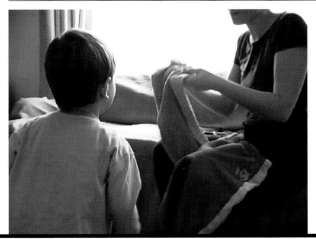

2 To make his choice easier, Julie has selected two sets of clothes, which she lays on her knees.

3 Julie asks Ethan: 'Which pair of trousers would you like to wear today?'

5 Julie places the red pair on the sofa.

6 Next, she holds up a T-shirt, which Ethan immediately chooses…

9 She draws him into conversation about the motif on the T-shirt he selected. By encouraging him, Julie supports his choice of clothes.

10 Ethan is now dressed, and shares his delight in his choice of outfit with Julie.

📽 *Picture story*   ETHAN 2 *years 3 months*

THE CONTINUING STRIVE FOR INDEPENDENCE

'Me do it', or 'I do it'

The phrase *'No,'* begins to be replaced by *'Me do it,'* which indicates that the striving for independence is ongoing. Children show great pleasure when a task is successfully completed, and intense frustration if they are unsuccessful. Once children realise they are capable of doing something by themselves, even with a varying degree of success, they may start to refuse adult help. What may seem to adults to be a routine task, such as putting on shoes or a coat, is a challenge for children that needs to be mastered. This can turn into a battle between parents and children, especially when time is of the essence, but it reflects the beginning of children's autonomy, of having a degree of control over 'their world'. This can be frustrating for adults who are in a hurry to go out, but it is an important stage in a child's development. It not only develops new skills but also boosts their self-confidence and fosters a growing sense of independence, both of which are needed in years to come.

1 Ethan and his brother, John, play together on the computer.

5 John takes the CD out of the sleeve and Ethan immediately takes hold of it. John says, *'OK, I'll let you do it.'*

Children must establish the fact that they have some sort of control in their lives. Completing a task for them, or suggesting a way to resolve a problem, may well be met with a frustrated outburst. It can be less stressful to think ahead and invite them to put on their shoes, or coat, before you are ready to go out. This will enable the child to try in their own time, and to ask for help if needed. Children need to struggle to succeed and parents need to accept this drive they have within themselves.

9 Ethan watches John as he puts the CD back in the plastic pocket. Ethan is learning an important final stage; putting a CD away.

10 Ethan says, *'Um... putting in...'*

11 *'...and shut the door.'* Ethan shows his competence by being able to carry out the action whilst looking at the screen.

Ethan loves to play on the computer, and he will insist that he puts a CD into the CD drive. By doing so, Ethan shows he has successfully learned the order of events that make it possible to play a CD on a computer. His confidence grows as he learns to do more.

2 John is not surprised when Ethan indicates he wants to put on a favourite CD.

3 John stops the activity on the computer.

4 Ethan selects, and points to the CD of his choice.

6 Ethan presses the button…

7 …and looks at the computer screen which displays the actions, whilst he passes the CD from one hand to the other.

8 Ethan removes John's CD and gives it to him.

12 He climbs up to sit on the chair…

13 …and when he is settled, tells John, *'Go on, go.'*

14 Ethan points to the curser and tells John, *'Go on that, it's dis.'* Ethan shows he has a clear understanding of what is happening.

RELATIONSHIPS: CHILD MINDERS AND CARERS

All-day care for children of working parents

The question of whether to return to work and when differs according to our individual circumstances, but whenever it occurs, by choice or not, it can be a stressful time. For some, the arrival of a baby is something to be fitted in around an already busy work schedule, causing a dilemma, as both career and family are equally important. For others, the financial strain of losing one, or the only income, leaves parents with no choice other than to return to work at the end of the statutory period of maternity and paternity leave, or even sooner.

The result is the same for everyone. Parents have to entrust the care of their children to others, whom they may not know well. Be it at home with a nanny or au pair, or leaving their child at a child-minder's or day-care centre, the quality of child care is all important. Children of working parents spend long periods of time with their carers, and form strong bonds with them (*see 'Attachments', page 120*), so the quality and continuity of care is more important than the amount of time they spend with carers.

It is reassuring for parents to know that high quality care can be of great benefit to children, who are able to enjoy a wide variety of experiences with different people and with children of a similar age. Parents know their children best and need to choose the most suitable care for them. Your local clinic or surgery should have plenty of information and can offer advice and support to those returning to work.

📽 *Picture story*
ROSALIND 2 years 1 month,
JAMIE 5 months, brother

Today is Sandra's first day back at work and she is feeling apprehensive at having to leave her two children with child minder, Kelly, for the first time. Rosalind has recently spent an hour with Kelly to help her become familiar with the house and the other children.

1 Rosalind is able to walk into Kelly's house by herself. Kelly holds her doll but Rosalind shows she needs her blanket for support.

2 Kelly holds Jamie, who is interested in the other children in the house. She is talking and makes contact with Rosalind who is in her mother's arms.

3 Rosalind is able to leave Sandra's arms, and is in the garden as Sandra says goodbye. Jamie is unperturbed and only seems fascinated by Megan.

Children form special relationships with their carers and other children, enjoying a range of activities and experiencing a varied spectrum of life.

4 Sandra waves goodbye, and Rosalind immediately runs after her.

5 As Rosalind realises her mother is leaving, she vocalises her protest.

6 Within minutes, Rosalind has settled down, and eats her breakfast with her doll close beside her.

📽 *Picture story*

STARTING NURSERY (1)

It was OK yesterday, but not today

Starting at nursery can be difficult for both children and parents; it is an important emotional step for the whole family, and a change in routine which can be upsetting. It is often the first time a child has been without the support of their prime carer. To be alone in a new place with unknown children, and to have to share the attention of unfamiliar adults, can prove to be very daunting. However, children are very different and their reactions vary. Some children run in happily without saying goodbye, others find the separation hard. Others cope one day but not the next, when they realise the experience is becoming a permanent routine.

Children's emotional uncertainties may bring about changes at home which seem out of character (*see 'Regression', page 101*). This is normal behaviour and shows that children need to revisit a more secure time in their lives before moving forward.

1 As Malachi reaches the nursery gate he becomes very upset.

5 Malachi screams in protest. Destiny moves on to another toy.

6 Malachi calms until Jayden decides he wants to play with the car.

7 Malachi looks to Kim and gets upset as he points to the car which Jayden is now driving away.

8 Kim then distracts Malachi by walking round the playground as she tries to interest him in an activity. But Malachi is too upset...

9 ...and wants to be picked up.

10 They chat to nursery teacher, Helen. Kim feels he is too unhappy to stay today. They all agree that Malachi managed well on his first session and he should try again next time.

MALACHI 2 *years 7 months*

On Malachi's first day at nursery, he ran and happily joined in the activities, with hardly a glance back at his mother, Kim. But today Malachi is not so keen.

2 Kim and nursery teacher, Ellen, listen to Malachi as he tries to express himself in words.

3 Unfortunately, at the moment, he seems too upset to be able to.

4 Kim decides to let Malachi's sister, Destiny, play. Kim talks to Malachi and tries to encourage him to join Destiny as she plays with a car.

11 With tears in his eyes, Malachi waves goodbye to Helen.

12 As Malachi leaves the nursery he is calm and runs his fingers along the railings. He looks back as the other children play; it will not be long before he too can stay.

🎬 *Picture story*

STARTING NURSERY (2)

Being able to let go – settling down in nursery

For some children, leaving their parents and joining in with activities and other children may come easily, but others can find the whole experience very traumatic – showing their distress by crying and clinging on to their parents for as long as they are able, until the inevitable parting.

Parents can find it emotionally draining to leave an unhappy child, and if on collection they are also greeted with tears, their worries will not be allayed, even after assurance from the nursery staff that the child settled down well. These 'welcome' tears show children's love and sense of relief at this emotional reunion with their parents: *'I've missed you and I'm glad you have returned,'* much the same as we do on being reunited with a loved one, after a long time apart.

ELIZABETH *2 years 7 months* ▸

Elizabeth finds it difficult to leave her mother, Nicola, when it is time for nursery. However, Elizabeth's older brother, Shane, is happy to play and does not want to leave when his sister is dropped off.

Nicola reassures Elizabeth that she will return to collect her. On returning, Nicola reminds Elizabeth that she did come back as she had promised.

3 Elizabeth is desperate to stay with Nicola and she holds on to her mother tightly. Nursery teacher, Ellen, steps in and takes Elizabeth, assuring her she will see her mother soon.

4 Ellen quickly takes Elizabeth inside and distracts her by suggesting they sit down together and roll some dough.

5 Ellen has captured Elizabeth's interest and she begins to calm a little.

9 Once all the parents have left, Elizabeth settles. With the support of a comforter, she is able to go outside. Ellen suggests they play a game.

10 Elizabeth joins in the game and is able to leave Ellen's arms.

11 Elizabeth now feels able to play with the sand, beside Felix. Ellen still remains in contact with Elizabeth as she watches the other children.

1 Elizabeth is upset, and although her mother, Nicola, tries to encourage her to play…

2 …Elizabeth still cries and clings to her mother, throwing her arms up to be picked up.

6 But Elizabeth sees her mother out of the window and she shows her distress.

7 Outside, Nicola is now having the opposite problem. She has difficulty persuading Shane he has to leave and that it is his turn tomorrow.

8 Ellen moves Elizabeth out of sight of her mother and brother. Ellen again tries to distract Elizabeth as she welcomes and introduces some other children who have just arrived.

12 Elizabeth is finally able to leave Ellen's side and, without the support of her comforter, enjoys blowing bubbles with Peter.

13 When she sees her mother at the end of nursery she runs to her, showing her emotions have returned.

14 Nicola and Elizabeth are reunited and Ellen tells Nicola what Elizabeth has been doing and how well she has managed.

📽 *Picture story*

THE BEGINNINGS OF RELATIONSHIPS WITH OTHER CHILDREN (1)

Making new friends when sharing is still difficult

PETER 2 *years 10 months,*
JAYDEN 2 *years 6 months*

Going to a nursery is an ideal way for children to meet and make new friends of their own age, but as they are still 'self-centred' at this age, it makes sharing extremely difficult for them (*see 'Favourite words', page 156, 'Empathy', page 282*).

As children start to interact, they begin to experience what it feels like when another child won't share. With limited communication skills, the resulting frustration can lead to conflict, and hitting, kicking or biting. It will not be until children are able to empathise and share, that they will realise that someone else can feel pain even if they do not experience it themselves.

1 Peter is playing with a toy car which Jayden decides he wants to play with. He attempts to put his hand on the car.

5 Jayden follows Peter and points to the large push-along cars. Helen stays nearby, observing how they manage this difficult new social skill – sharing.

6 Jayden goes directly to the push-along cars. Peter decides to go over to the bench.

7 Jayden looks around for Peter.

11 Jayden brings Peter's attention to the horn.

12 Jayden then spots the original toy car which Peter still has. He shouts his frustration as he opens the door of the push-along car.

13 Peter makes an attempt to bite Jayden, but Helen intervenes…

Peter and Jayden show they have not yet learned to share the toy car, but they are starting to communicate with each other. In doing so, they find that they share a common interest – cars.

2 Peter quickly picks up the car and runs away with it. In his frustration, Jayden shouts out to nursery teacher, Helen, for support; Helen remains near, but does not feel she needs to intervene.

3 Jayden runs after Peter and calls out, *'Peter.'* He turns round towards Jayden...

4 ...and then runs off again. Peter shows he is enjoying the start of a chasing game: Jayden is not so sure.

8 Helen shows Jayden where Peter is.

9 Peter is already sitting in the car and Jayden places his hand on the wheel.

10 Jayden indicates to Peter that the wheel can go round. Together, they turn the wheel, as Helen continues to observe.

14 ...and sensitively guides Peter and Jayden as she reminds them of the concepts of 'sharing' and saying 'sorry'.

15 At the end of nursery, Jayden shows interest and looks on as Peter waves and says *'Goodbye'* to Helen.

16 Jayden then says, *'Goodbye'* and waves to Peter as he leaves, showing the beginnings of a friendship.

▣ *Picture story*

THE BEGINNINGS OF RELATIONSHIPS WITH OTHER CHILDREN (2)

Difficulties with communication: learning a second language

Although children play alongside each other (*see 'Parallel play', page 206*), they are beginning to show an interest in interacting with each other, which they do by making use of their emerging communication skills. However, for some children living in the UK, English is not their native language, which makes it even more difficult and frustrating for them and their carers. Their emerging communication skills are of little help to them in situations where sharing and conflicts become an issue, and they need extra support from their carers.

JAYDEN 2 *years 6 months,* FELIX 2 *years 8 months*

1 Jayden approaches Felix. He has a shovel in his hand ready to play in the sand pit.

5 ...their nursery teacher, Helen, intervenes. She removes Jayden's shovel as she supports Felix. This time Jayden is able to cope on his own and finds another activity.

6 Upset, Felix turns to the sandpit. He strikes the bucket as he vents his frustration.

7 When Peter comes to fill his bucket with sand, Felix throws his head back showing an extreme emotion, saying, '*Niet, niet.*' ('No, no.')

11 A little later, Helen decides to get out Gerald, the guinea pig. Felix has been showing an interest, but when Jayden nears to stroke Gerald...

12 ...Felix becomes upset once more. Again, Helen reassures him.

13 Felix settles and is even able to accept Peter's approach, when he comes to feed Gerald.

Felix has very recently moved to the UK from Russia and has no English language. This makes it even more difficult for him to communicate with those around him and to form friendships with his peers.

2 Jayden talks to Felix, who is unable to understand what Jayden is saying. Felix stands up and mimics Jayden, putting his shovel up to Jayden's.

3 Jayden pushes his shovel towards Felix.

4 They both strike out at each other, and Felix cries out. Unable to resolve the situation themselves....

8 As he cries, Felix points and talks in his native tongue. Although Helen doesn't understand what he is trying to tell her, she reassures him.

9 Helen then distracts Felix by gesturing that he can blow some bubbles. Felix indicates he wants to.

10 Felix is calm again as he happily blows bubbles.

14 Towards the end of nursery, Felix is able to tolerate Jayden as he plays near him in the sandpit. Helen stays close by.

15 Jayden then helps to fill Felix's bucket. Helen praises them both...

16 ...and leaves them to continue playing 'together'.

COMMUNICATION

Learning the structure of language, categorising into smaller groups and the association of symbols

Children are beginning to put words together when they speak. These first attempts at sentences are not made up of random words, but show that children are beginning to understand that the order in which they are used makes a difference to their meaning, eg *'help me,'* and *'me help.'* The rules of language are complex, but children are learning them at a remarkable rate, and listening to general conversation helps their vocabulary and sentence construction. It is at this stage that adults need to use appropriate language themselves! Children can get so excited when joining in a conversation that they may start to stutter. If this happens and the child continues to struggle to tell the story, adults may need to sensitively fill in essential gaps. This not only encourages conversation but marks the start of being able to see life from the child's point of view.

Children love picture books and can now recognise what is living and what is not, mainly based on whether it moves or not. They also begin to distinguish between different breeds of one type of animal and can categorise other types of animals, even if they haven't seen them in reality.

Children now begin to draw vertical and horizontal lines, and circles. These images can then be related to what they see around them. They can also show the correct number of fingers when given a simple number but at this age they have not learned what 'numbers' mean.

JAYDEN *2 years 6 month* studies a picture book.

ETHAN *2 years 3 months* chats away to himself, practising his language skills.

Ethan's sister, Katie, has asked him a question. ETHAN *2 years 3 months* says, *'Umm'* and looks about as he carefully considers his answer.

Katie smiles as she patiently waits for Ethan's reply. She lets him take his time and doesn't hurry him.

Katie understands it is also important that she listens to his reply. It will help her gain an insight into Ethan's world; his likes and dislikes, his thoughts and his feelings.

Ethan's greater understanding of language and his improving communication skills mean that he and Katie can share more things together.

📽 *Picture story*

ETHAN *2 years 3 months*

Ethan is now able to not only draw shapes (2D) from his imagination, but also hold the images in his memory and relate them to real objects (3D) in the world around him.

1 Ethan starts to draw. He has picked up a pen in his left hand and tries to draw.

2 He changes to his preferred right hand to continue. His mother, Julie, asks him to draw a triangle.

3 Ethan draws a triangle – and a circle…

4 …before deciding to draw around his hand.

5 Ethan does not find this easy and Julie asks if he needs help. Ethan replies, '*No.*'

6 In the playground, after his siblings have gone into school, Ethan puts his foot on the number 1. It is in a triangular shape and Ethan says, '*Triangle.*'

7 He then goes to the number 2 and stands in the circular shape and says, '*Circle.*'

8 Ethan points to the netball hoop and says, '*Circle.*'

📽 *Picture story*

I KNOW NOW

'I can tell you'

As children begin to understand rules, and the meaning of what is right and wrong, they can start to think ahead about the consequences of their actions.

Children are also quick to notice when someone else is doing something wrong and they are not afraid to point it out!

ELIZABETH *2 years 7 months*

1 Elizabeth happily starts a picture.

5 Elizabeth quickly points out, *'Not there...'*

6 *'...Here.'*

10 Elizabeth emphasises her disapproval of Ellen's previous marks in three different ways; first by pointing, then by saying, *'Not there.'...*

11 ...and finally, by touching the pen mark with her fingers.

2 Nursery teacher, Ellen, writes Elizabeth's name on the picture.

3 Elizabeth cannot seem to make a pen work and offers it to Ellen…

4 …who tries the pen out on the newspaper so as not to mark the picture.

7 Ellen explains that she didn't want to spoil Elizabeth's lovely picture.

8 Elizabeth gives Ellen another pen…

9 …and this time Ellen tries out the pen in the corner of Elizabeth's picture.

12 '*Drawing for my mummy, mummy.*' She looks in the direction her mummy will come to collect her from nursery.

13 This is Elizabeth's special drawing of an elephant. We may not understand such drawings, but they have real meaning to our children.

LEARNING THROUGH PLAY

🎥 *Picture story*

BEGINNING TO BRING ORDER INTO 'THEIR WORLD'

As children begin to learn that there are everyday routines, and that one event follows another – we wake up, wash, get dressed, and then eat breakfast, and so on, they start to apply this to what they see around them. With increased concentration and improved motor skills, children can begin to show their need to impose more order in their life. Being able to sort and categorise events and activities helps children to make more sense of the things in 'their world'. Repeating sequences in the correct order means children become less involved in random activity, and their lives become more purposeful.

ETHAN 2 *years 3 months*

1 Ethan pulls out a large towel from the washing basket.

5 He passes it to Julie, who puts it on the worktop.

JAYDEN 2 *years 6 months*
Jayden shows that he knows there should be a railway engine at the front of a line of carriages.

1 Jayden has picked up an orange engine and a carriage. He approaches the train.

2 He removes a red carriage and replaces it with the orange engine.

Ethan loves to help his mother, Julie, to fold up the washing.

2 He shakes it vigorously...

3 ...before using his legs to roll it.

4 As he reaches the floor, the towel is completely rolled up.

6 Ethan returns to the basket and pulls out another article, and once again, shakes it vigorously.

7 Again he rolls it up against his body.

8 This time places it on the worktop himself. He looks to Julie, who claps and praises his efforts.

3 He then adds two carriages in front of the green engine.

4 Jayden then removes the green engine...

5 ...and places it at the front again.

📽 *Picture story*

LEARNING ABOUT THE WORLD AROUND THEM

The quest for greater understanding

Children still have much to learn and discover about the world around them and they continue to do so with enthusiasm.

As their use and understanding of language progresses and they can put words together to make simple sentences, they are able to improve their knowledge. Children's favourite questions *'What's this?'*, *'Who's that?'* and *'Why?'* become commonly used in their quest for knowledge.

ETHAN *2 years 3 months*

1 Ethan looks at the drinking fountain and says, *'Water.'*

RAE *3 years* with her care-worker, Sharon, discovers the sensation of touching a starfish.

ETHAN *2 years 3 months* works out that the only way he can look up at a plane in the sky when the sun is in his eyes, is by squinting and sheilding one eye.

PETER *2 years 10 months* investigates what is on the leaves.

JASMIN *2 years 11 months* explores the properties of light and shade.

Ethan's mother, Julie, is becoming aware that Ethan is fascinated by how things work, and sometimes finds his questions are hard to explain.

2 He then goes over to the drain-pipe and peers down the drain saying, '*Water.*'

3 Ethan looks back to the drinking fountain, showing that he has related the two together...

4 ...but as he gazes up and follows the path of the drain-pipe, he is not yet able to understand the connection.

FELIX *2 years 8 months* samples some dough to see what it tastes like.

KIERON *3 years* is both absorbed and delighted by the light shining through bottles of coloured water.

ELIZABETH *2 years 7 months* is fascinated by the see-through toy car. She pushes it backwards and forwards along the worktop and gazes at the coloured cogs inside as they go round and round.

📽 *Picture story*

PROBLEM-SOLVING

Becoming less frustrated

The combination of better concentration, patience and physical ability enables children to order and start to problem-solve for themselves.

To find a problem, and then be able to solve it takes a lot of planning and forward thinking. Trial and error, cause and effect and determination are still used to learn how to find the best solution.

JAYDEN 2 *years 6 months*

1 Jayden is on the green trike. He bumps into the red one and attempts to pull it out the way. But the red trike is on a slope and keeps slipping away from him.

2 Jayden decides to get off the green trike...

6 Jayden has got off the green trike and pushed it out of the way. He now decides to get on the red trike.

7 He drives the trike through the gap, but as he does, he gets the wheel tangled with the leg of the chalk board.

FELIX 2 *years 8 months*   *Felix has recently moved to the UK from Russia and speaks no English. However, he demonstrates that when shown what to do, he learns quickly.*

1 Felix has just finished his picture.

2 He cannot get the drawing off the board, and as he tries and pulls at it, he rips the paper.

3 He is able to show nursery teacher, Ellen, what has happened...

*Jayden wants to pass, with his trike, through the gap between the
table and the chalk board.*

3 ...and pulls the red trike right out of the way.

4 Jayden returns and gets back on the green trike.

5 But as he heads towards the gap he touches the red trike which slides down the slope with him.

8 Jayden once again gets off the trike and tries to release the trike's wheel.

9 He returns to the trike and negotiates his way.

10 Jayden has successfully managed to drive the trike through the gaps on his own, even if this time, it was not on the bike of his choice.

4 ...and she demonstrates that the clip has to be squeezed together in order for it to release the paper.

5 Felix completes another picture and is now able to remove the clip himself...

6 ...and put it back on to the board for next time.

BECOMING AWARE OF SELF

🎥 *Picture story*

I AM GETTING TO KNOW WHO I AM

Improving awareness of self and others

Children can now begin to recognise themselves physically in a photograph, both as they are now and when they were a baby. This shows that children have developed an awareness of the past and that living things can grow, ie they themselves were once a baby and they have now grown. However, they still believe everyone can see what they see.

Time, though, is still based on experience – the order of events throughout the day; and association – when visiting a friend's house children know it is time to go home only when they are leaving. Children do not understand phrases such as *'Hurry up, we'll be late,'* or *'In a minute,'* as they have yet to learn what time means.

ETHAN *2 years 3 months*

Although Ethan can now recognise himself as a baby, he has trouble with naming his older siblings when they were younger.

ETHAN *2 years 3 months*

Ethan points out his brother and sisters to his mother, Julie. As he does, he tries using his fingers to point in various ways.

1 Julie asks, *'Who's that?'* Ethan points to each face in the photograph and says: *'Jessica,'*

2 *'Daniel,'*

ETHAN *2 years 3 months*

Although Ethan can recognise himself as a baby, he still assumes everyone can see what he is looking at.

Ethan is on the phone to his grandma.

1 Ethan tells his grandma about a drawing he has just done…

2 …and holds it up for her to see.

1 Ethan shows he knows it is himself when he was a baby in the photo sequence in *The Social Baby*.

2 However, when he looks at a photograph of his sister, Kelly, when she was younger, he says it is his brother, John.

3 He makes no mistake about knowing his mother and father.

3 *'Tiffany,'*

4 *'Boysie.'* (Boysie is Ethan's own name for himself, which the family now use.)

5 Julie asks Ethan, *'Where's Boysie's nose?'* Ethan points to his nose in the photograph, using his little finger.

3 Ethan points to the triangle.

4 He also waves to her as they say *'Bye…*

5 *…bye.'*

SECTION FIVE

THE FOURTH YEAR
AND PRESCHOOL

PHYSICAL DEVELOPMENT

As children's physical ability develops so does their confidence. They are now able to go up and down stairs alone, climb ladders, use the pedals on a tricycle, run and turn sharply in another direction, hop, stand and run on tip-toes and also sit cross-legged.

🎥 *Picture story*

OLIVER *3 years 9 months*
Oliver shows how physically able he is and that he has learned to judge space and distance accurately.

JAMES *3 years 11 months,*
OLIVER *3 years 9 months,*
RHIANNA *4 years 6 months*

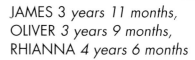

1 James and Oliver have been running around the playground together. They spot Rhianna...

LAURANCE *3 years 11 months*

1 Laurance has decided to run as fast as he can towards the drum.

1 Oliver springs from a stepping stone…

2 …to a hop-scotch mat, landing with both feet in the starting position.

3 Oliver needs to use all his concentration to retain his balance, as he enthusiastically proceeds to hop-scotch along the mat.

2 …and run off together. Rhianna chases after the boys, but decides to change direction suddenly. She stops in her tracks…

3 …and twists herself round. She is able to keep her momentum as she runs off in the opposite direction.

4 Rhianna's tactic works and she catches Oliver. A game of 'tag' begins.

2 He hurls himself at the drum with such force that it lifts off the ground.

3 He throws his leg over the drum and twists, as he grabs the front.

4 Using all his strength, Laurance successfully manages to sit astride the drum.

FINE MOTOR SKILLS

Dexterity

Children can manage with ease the skills they practise and repeat every day: they are able to dress and undress, wash and dry their hands, and brush their teeth. However, children are also beginning to learn more complex tasks, such as using scissors and threading beads, which require greater concentration and improved hand/eye co-ordination. Children remain determined to achieve success without any adult help and so may still become frustrated on occasions.

📽 *Picture story*

ABIGAIL *4 years*

Abigail enjoys threading buttons and beads. Today, she uses a shoe-lace to thread a button: she passes the lace back and forth, showing she will soon be able to extend her skill to sewing.

Children display their improved fine motor skills when carrying out everyday activities, and in play.

SIAN *3 years 8 months*

Sian is using scissors to cut up some dough. She is learning about properties by cutting a material other than paper.

1 Sian is standing and has lifted up the dough. She studies it as she places the scissors to begin to cut a piece off.

2 She observes the scissors and the dough as she cuts.

1 Abigail has started to thread the button. She has passed the lace through once and with her right finger and thumb, is pushing it through the next hole.

2 Abigail turns the button over, enabling the fingers of her left hand to catch...

3 ...and pull the lace through.

4 Abigail passes the lace to her right hand once again. She is totally absorbed in the activity and shows her concentration as she tips her head to the side.

5 She has successfully found the next hole in the button...

6 ...and pulls through the lace. Abigail has been able to thread the button calmly and confidently without becoming frustrated or needing help.

3 As she closes the scissors to complete a cut, the weight of the dough makes it fall.

4 Sian has confirmed her understanding of gravity, and looks to where the dough has dropped. Without feeling the need to pick up the dropped piece...

5 ...she carries on using the scissors. Sian presses them against her hand showing that this time she is anticpating when the dough will fall.

RELATIONSHIPS AND INDEPENDENCE

Around this time children, are becoming more confident and better able to accept separation, though many will still need reassurance. There is rapid development of children's memory, which makes it easier for them to believe a loved one has not gone for ever, and will return.

Children become more co-operative, starting to understand that others have thoughts and feelings of their own and learning to empathise. This helps them to be tolerant, and, with improving memory and attention span, better able to follow instructions and be involved in group activity.

Though by no means all the time, boys and girls become interested in gender-based activities and start to choose to play with children of the same sex. With higher levels of testosterone, boys are physically unable to remain still for long periods of time, and will tend to group together, running around and being 'boisterous'; whereas girls are more likely to pair off and play quieter, more ordered activities.

HERMIONE *3 years 11 months*

CARA *3 years 1 month*

LAURENCE *3 years 5 months*

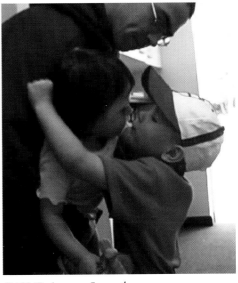

SHANE *4 years 5 months*

SERINDA
3 years 1 month

SHENALI *4 years 1 month,*
LAURA *3 years 9 months*

SHAYAN *4 years 7 months,*
JEROME *4 years 8 months,*
KALLUM *3 years 7 months*

MICHAEL *4 years 4 months,*
SHANE *4 years 5 months,*
OLIVER *3 years 9 months,*
FINN *3 years 6 months*

COMMUNICATION

📽 *Picture story*

INTERRUPTING TO GAIN ATTENTION

Children of this age continually ask questions; though the answers often seem unimportant, with the child losing interest, or asking another question before the first has been answered. Often, their questions require an answer that is beyond their comprehension, and it is more their need to improve social and language skills which is important. Children's eagerness to join in may sometimes be their only motivation, and once involved in a conversation, they may not have anything to say. This does not stop them from trying though, and interrupting adults when they are in conversation becomes common practice.

Children still live for 'now', and use various methods to get their parents' attention when they are talking; trying to physically pull them away, standing between the two parties, singing, making a noise, or putting a hand over the parents or other person's mouth. Parents can encourage children to say 'excuse me' rather than interrupting. When children do, they should not be kept waiting for too long, because although their memory is improving, they often forget what it was they wanted to say in the first place.

CARA *3 years 1 month*
Cara does not like it when her mother, Ceri's, attention is taken away from her, especially when Ceri is talking on the phone.

4 Cara starts to become frustrated as Ceri carries on talking and ignoring her. Cara again prods her mother, and decides she wants to talk to her grandmother.

ABIGAIL *4 years*
Abigail often forgets what she wants to say and finds it frustrating when she cannot get her mother, Kerry's, immediate attention. However, when she does, she will manage to talk about something even if it was not what she had planned.

1 Kerry is chatting to a friend and Abigail has got the family album out to look at. She has spotted something in a photograph.

2 She tries to get Kerry's attention first by talking and then by shaking her shoulder. Both approaches have not worked, and Kerry is still talking.

1 Ceri is on the phone, talking to Cara's grandmother. Cara starts to chat to Ceri as she climbs up on the sofa.

2 Ceri ignores Cara, who turns her back and tries to entertain herself with her doll.

3 But she cannot, and turns to Ceri, prodding her arm and talking.

5 Cara attempts to pull the phone away. As Ceri is talking to Cara's grandmother, she decides this time Cara can have the phone.

6 Cara listens as her grandmother asks her what she has been doing today. Cara tells her that she played in the sand and is going to have a bath.

7 After a short time, Cara hands the phone back to Ceri. Cara is now able to play quietly beside her mother while she continues her conversation.

3 Next, Abigail walks around to face Kerry. With her back to the friend, she attempts to gain eye contact with Kerry and her attention.

4 Finally, Abigail physically turns Kerry's head to face her.

5 Abigail has successfully got Kerry's attention. She has forgotten what she originally wanted to say, but points to another photograph and talks.

WORDS AND SYMBOLS

Communicating thoughts and ideas from memory

At this age, children's art is becoming more purposeful. They are now able to say in advance what they are going to draw or paint and choose different media to illustrate their pictures. Children may also provide a commentary as they carry out their ideas. Although the original idea may change as they proceed with the picture, it shows that children started with a preconceived visual image in their minds and they are able to transfer this to paper. A similar process happens when children make up a song or a piece of music.

HAIBATU *3 years 5 months* has put large blue chalk marks on the paper and now she is rubbing them with her hand. She is discovering the effect this will have.

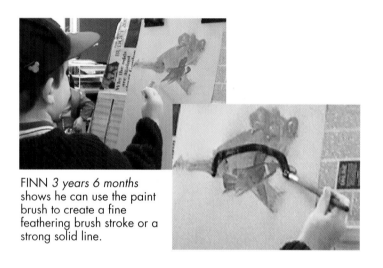

FINN *3 years 6 months* shows he can use the paint brush to create a fine feathering brush stroke or a strong solid line.

HERMIONE *3 years 11 months* paints confidently, covering the whole of the paper.

🎥 *Picture story*

SIAN *3 years 8 months*

Sian is drawing a person. As she draws, she says in advance which part of the person she is going to add next. This shows she is able to think ahead.

1 Sian begins to draw carefully. She is using a pencil very competently and with her preferred hand.

2 Sian does not need to look for reminders of what a person looks like: she is recalling the image from her memory.

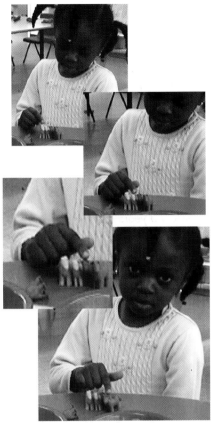

ABIGAIL *4 years* looks at a book with her mother, Kelly. Although she cannot yet read, she knows the words tell a story related to the pictures. At the moment she tells her own story using the pictures in the book.

FINN *3 years 6 months* is able to use the mouse on a computer. His nursery teacher, Helen, encourages him to explore other elements of the programme by himself.

HAIBATU *3 years 5 months* and ABIGAIL *4 years* are both showing they can count. They are beginning to understand about numbers and that they have meaning.

3 Sian surveys her drawing, checking that she has included all the elements. She shows her attention to detail.

4 When Sian has finished, she turns the picture towards us, so we can see too. By doing this, Sian shows she knows that just because she can see her picture, it does not necessarily mean others can too.

5 Sian's picture of a person.

EMPATHY

Understanding how others feel

Only when children have learned that other people have feelings of their own, can they start to show concern for the well-being of others. They will then not only be able to share their feelings, but also their possessions.

Friendships are valuable, as they enable children to experience a range of feelings and emotions such as warmth, love and happiness. On occasions though, children may feel anger or jealousy, and learning to resolve these emotions helps children gain a sense of empathy. When someone cries, especially a close friend, children who can understand the feelings of another show compassion. After consoling the friend, children often try to cheer them up and make them 'better' again. This form of empathy strengthens friendships and helps build new ones.

If someone is hurt, or upset, younger children may empathise by offering the person a comforter of their own, or something inappropriate that they themselves would be comforted by. An older child may come down to a younger age-level, or speak using 'motherese', as a mother does to a baby.

Picture story

ROSALIND *2 years 7 months,* ABIGAIL *4 years*

Today is Rosalind's first day with her child minder.

SYDNEY *4 years 2 months* and EMILY *4 years 5 months* greet each other at nursery by giving each other a reassuring hug.

HAIBATU *3 years 5 months,* RHIANNA *4 years 6 months*

1 Haibatu fell over on her way to nursery this morning. As she is playing, she touches her knee, which is still sore.

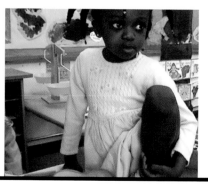

2 Haibatu holds up her knee...

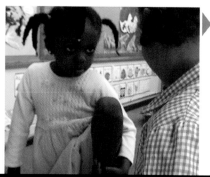

3 ...and tells her story to Rhianna.

1 Rosalind is upset that her mother Sandra is leaving.

2 Abigail has heard Rosalind and has brought out Rosalind's special blanket and doll.

3 Rosalind takes her comforters and hugs them for support. Abigail has shown she can understand what Rosalind is feeling and has thought about what Rosalind needs to comfort herself.

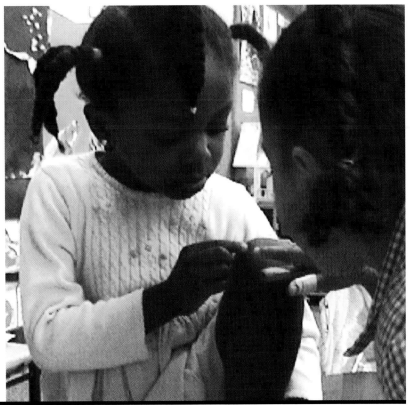

4 Rhianna looks closely at Haibatu's injured knee and asks where it hurts.

5 Haibatu points to the injury and Rhianna sympathises. Rhianna tells Haibatu she hurt her thumb the other day. Both girls are learning to 'feel' what it was like for the other.

LEARNING THROUGH PLAY

🎥 *Picture story*

SECRETS AND IMAGINARY PLAY

Children are only now beginning to learn that other people have minds of their own, with thoughts, feelings and ideas that are different from theirs, and over which they have no control. This is one of the hardest of human concepts for children to grasp, but once they have, it opens up a whole new world for them – and one which adults take for granted.

At this age, children's memory improves dramatically, making them much better able to retain and recall images and events. This ability means sophisticated imaginary play is possible. They can now play 'let's pretend' games together – known as 'joint pretence'. This involves having the ability to suspend belief in the reality of an object, and pretend it is something else – and then hold that pretence in their memory. For example, two children may have a stick and a stone: one child pretends the stick is a plane, and the other pretends the stone is a car. To play the game successfully, each child needs to be able to hold these different views of each object in their minds, and at the same time. The fact that they are able to do this shows children are becoming aware that other people have minds of their own, and they are learning to see things from another's point of view.

With this ability, children realise they can change reality by imposing their own imagination on events, and see the world from any viewpoint, using any objects and pretence they choose. This is a big step towards understanding what other people are thinking – and reading other people's minds.

SYDNEY *4 years 2 months,*
CHRISTOPHER *4 years 5 months*

1 Sydney and Christopher are playing with the sand. She sees us, and whispers, *'I've got a secret to tell you.'*

CARA *3 years 1 month,*
HANNAH *8 years*

Cara is playing a pretend game with her sister's friend, Hannah. Cara now understands they have separate minds. She is able to pretend without the use of any props, showing she has the ability to hold images in her mind, and recall them at will, whilst at the same time, visualise what others imagine.

1 Cara automatically assumes that Hannah is able to play the game. Cara looks at Hannah and starts by holding out the palm of her hand.

2 Cara imagines it's a phone and taps in some numbers. She also makes the appropriate sound, which alerts Hannah to what is about to happen.

Sydney has a secret to share with Christopher. They have learned to whisper and show they understand that even though they know the secret, we will not, until we are told. They no longer assume that we know everything they do.

2 Sydney gets closer to Christopher and whispers something.

3 Christopher's says, 'Arhh.'...

4 ...and peers round to look at us, smiling.

CARA 3 *years 1 month*

Cara shows she has learned, and understands, when we can see an object, and when we cannot.

1 Cara hides her bottle of milk behind her back and says, '*You can't see it...*'

2 '*...You can now.*'

3 Cara continues, saying, '*Ring ring.*' Hannah puts her hand to her ear, as she too pretends she is holding a phone, and says: '*Hello.*'

4 Cara asks Hannah some questions; she listens to Hannah's replies and is able to converse coherently.

5 Cara shows she is able to visualise what Hannah has said and can reply by recalling the conversation and holding the image in her mind.

STORIES, HUMOUR AND TRUTHFULNESS

Using imagination

Using their imagination helps children to enhance and elaborate their story-telling. When presented with make-believe stories such as nursery rhymes, cartoons and films, in books and on television, children find it difficult to distinguish between what is fantasy and what is fact. They have yet to become able to understand the subtleties of the spoken word or to read body language.

As children start to take an interest in conversation, they will hear adults talking about events that they themselves have experienced. They may hear adults embellishing a story or introducing humour – something that is not yet possible for children of this age to fully comprehend. This marks the beginning of them learning about the complex and subtle language used in social interaction: what makes others laugh, and the concept of humour; how it is used and when it is appropriate. They have yet to learn to predict others words or actions correctly in order to know if someone is joking, or telling the truth or not.

Children also hear adults stretching the truth – telling 'white lies' to avoid hurting the feelings of others, something else children of this age cannot do. They are very honest and are unable to lie or deceive, which can be embarrassing for parents when their child points out the obvious in a loud voice: *'That man over there only has one eye. Why?'*

Like any other activity, telling a story takes practice, and children learn from the responses of others to their attempts. Signs that children are becoming aware are when they tell the most amazing stories, which they claim are true.

ABIGAIL *4 years* enjoys telling her mother stories. She is just realising she can make those around her laugh if she makes funny sounds and pulls faces. She is beginning to understand humour.

🎥 *Picture story*

ABIGAIL *4 years*

1 Abigail is given a hairband and asked to hide it in one of her hands.

5 When asked to say, *'Which hand is it in?'* she smiles, and touches her right hand.

ABIGAIL *4 years*

Abigail loves to play 'Hide-and-seek' and now understands the game. However, Abigail does not have the ability to hide herself completely. She still believes that because she cannot see us, we cannot see her.

Abigail is asked to hide a hairband in her hand. She automatically assumes that because she knows the answer, we must too. Her understanding of the way minds work, makes her unable to lie.

2 She prepares as she puts both hands behind her back.

3 Abigail brings our her right hand (in which she has hidden the hairband), and looks at it intently. She has immediately 'given the game away.'

4 Abigail brings out her other hand and, rather uneasily, presents them both.

6 Abigail shows she cannot suspend the truth, and answers her own question with complete honesty, by pointing to her hand.

7 When she holds out her hands once more, she gives us another clue by holding her right hand out in front of the other.

8 Finally, Abigail reveals the hand in which she is hiding the hairband. She is unable to carry out the deception. Abigail shows she has not yet learned to lie.

1 Abigail pulls a cushion from the chair and buries her face in it. She thinks she is hidden.

2 She cannot resist peeping out...

3 ...and is delighted when she is unexpectedly found!

📽 *Picture story*

BECOMING MORE CO-OPERATIVE (1)

Sharing and tolerance

Children learn what is acceptable, what is not, and their social skills from parents, family and other adults. With their peers, children try out what they each have learned; they test each other's boundaries and see the response.

Children's use of language and their ability to express themselves is improving, and this reduces their sense of frustration and tendency to have tantrums. An improving memory enables children to draw on past experience to solve problems, so they become better able to manage their behaviour.

RHIANNA *4 years 6 months,*
ZAKK *3 years 9 months,*
JONNY *3 years 10 months*

The children are playing with the dough; their nursery teacher, Rachel, is there to help. Jonny and Zakk are able to resolve a potential dispute about a plastic knife, without Rachel's intervention.

1 Rhianna, Rachel and Zakk are playing with the dough. Zakk is showing Rachel what he is making.

4 Rachel asks Zakk, *'Can Jonny have a go?'* She waits, as Zakk thinks.

7 Before Rachel returns, Jonny throws the knife back towards Zakk…

8 …who picks it up. Both Jonny and Zakk avoid eye contact at this point.

2 Jonny reaches over and picks up a plastic knife which Zakk has been using.

3 Zakk shouts, *'That's mine.'* Rachel confirms this by saying, *'Jonny, that's actually Zakk's from home.'*

5 He repeats, *'It's mine.'* Rachel confirms this: *'I know it's yours,'* adding, *'Can you share it?'* Zakk remains calm as he watches Jonny using his knife, but says nothing.

6 Rachel asks Zakk, *'Shall I get Jonny a different one?'* Zakk still does not reply. Rachel decides it would be the best option, and leaves to find another knife.

9 Zakk chuckles, and smiling, now makes eye contact with Jonny. Rhianna joins in.

10 Jonny smiles back and shows Zakk the scissors he has picked up. Rhianna calls Rachel to say that Zakk has his knife back now.

BECOMING MORE CO-OPERATIVE (2)

Taking turns and being helpful

By this age, children have more control over their own emotions and they start to understand how their actions can affect others, and vise versa. By observing whether an action was accidental or has been done intentionally, children can take the circumstances into account and judge how to respond to the situation.

Together with improved language skills, children are becoming more co-operative, considerate and prepared to help others. Children enjoy helping around the home and imitating adult activities. Giving children simple, attainable tasks to do, such as helping to lay the table, or dusting, encourages participation in family life and raises children's self-esteem and sense of belonging. Playing board games together helps children learn about sharing, waiting, and taking turns, all of which are useful skills for the future.

♣ *Picture story*

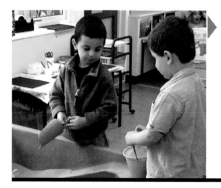

1 Oliver brings a bucket of sand to the sand pit. James has a scoop...

5 Next, Oliver finds his own scoop and together they pour sand into the bucket.

SHENALI *4 years 1 month,* OLIVER *3 years 9 months*

1 Shenali looks at the children playing with the dough. As Oliver rolls his piece of dough, it slips from his hands...

ABIGAIL *4 years* is able to take turns when playing a board game with her mother, Kelly. She is happy to play the game, but she may find not winning difficult to accept.

Abigail also enjoys dusting and imitating other household activities.

JAMES *3 years 11 months,*
OLIVER *3 years 9 months*

James and Oliver start to play together by co-operating and sharing an activity. James uses his ability to assess Oliver's actions when some sand is sprayed close to his face.

2 ...which he uses to pour some sand into the bucket.

3 Oliver shows his approval as he pats the top of the sand.

4 Oliver finds a shell with some sand in, and pours it into James' scoop.

6 As Oliver pats the sand with his scoop, he unknowingly sprays some sand in the air, very close to James' face.

7 James takes a step back and looks at Oliver, who is unaware of what has happened, and does not react. James accepts that Oliver's action was not deliberate...

8 ...and together they carry on enjoying their activities with the sand.

Shenalia shows she is able to be both co-operative and helpful.

2 ...and falls to the floor. Shenali turns and sees it land. Oliver looks to the ground to try to see where it has gone.

3 Shenali bends down and picks it up for Oliver...

4 ...and gives it to him.

📽 *Picture story*

BEGINNINGS OF SPECIAL FRIENDSHIPS

With rapidly improving memory, better language skills and an increasing awareness that others have minds of their own, children are able to communicate and play together more successfully. Relationships with their peers form an important part of this, enabling children to find out about themselves and others, develop friendships and learn about different patterns of behaviour. This helps shape children's moral judgment and beliefs.

LAURA *3 years 9 months,*
ZAKK *3 years 9 months,*
EMILY *4 years 5 months*

Laura and Zakk begin to role-play with some miniature people.

4 Laura replies, '...Ooh,...doh,...you boys.'

5 Zakk responds, holding up each of his people in turn, for them to say, 'I didn't do that,... I didn't do that,... I didn't do that.'

9 Laura: *'This is sister's.'* Zakk: *'The baby done it.'* Laura: *'No... it wasn't the baby.'*

10 Zakk: *'It was.'*
Emily tries to join in with a similar toy.

11 Laura: *'Yes it was...'* and then says to Emily, *'You're not play with us.'* Zakk confirms this as he takes the toy from Emily.

1 Laura starts the game, saying: *'Got to make darling a drink.'*

2 There is a moment's silence, until Zakk looks to the tree...

3 ...*'Look, all the leaves come off.'*

6 Laura: *'You did.'* Zakk: *'I didn't.'*

7 Laura: *'He did it.'*

8 Zakk: *'He didn't.'* Meanwhile, Emily, who is listening to the game, indicates she would like to join in.

12 Zakk and Laura move to another table to get some more toys. Together, they help each other gather the toys. Emily remains a bystander.

13 Zakk and Laura carry the toys back...

14 ...and continue to play. Emily loses interest in their game, but she remains close by, and happily plays a similar game of her own.

PRETEND PLAY (1)
Role play

A child of this age knows if he is a boy, or she is a girl, but this does not have a great deal of significance beyond labelling. Children have been identifying gender by categorisation and applying rules, which adults may find to be extremely sexist, but it is based on observation and experience; so it is logical for a child to assume all doctors are men and all nurses are women, if that is all they have seen.

Whilst not all games are gender-based, boys and girls are becoming more interested in identifying with gender-based activity, rather than simply mimicking adult behaviour; and their play begins to reflect more about what they see as being relevant to male or female. Children will dress up as mummy or daddy, doctors, nurses etc, and will alter their voices and accents as they mimic role-play. However, this does not mean they understand what it is like to be that person.

🎥 *Picture story*

1 Shane has come to Sian and Michael's shop. Sian grabs the till roll.

JONNY *3 years 10 months,* DOUGLAS *4 years 4 months*

1 Jonny opens the oven door and looks in.

MICHAEL *4 years 4 months,* OLIVER *3 years 9 months* and GUSTAV *3 years 10 months* are playing a pretend game together. Oliver and Gustav have put on hats and Oliver assumes the role of a male, using his voice in a low tone to emphasise he is a man.

5 Whilst Douglas looks in another cupboard, Jonny begins to tear off pieces of pizza with his hands.

SHANE *4 years 5 months,*
SIAN *3 years 8 months,*
MICHAEL *4 years 4 months*

Shane, Sian and Michael are playing shops. They assume the roles of shopkeepers and customer, and happily play the game using the elements they understand about shopping.

2 She tears some off and hands it to Shane. Michael opens his book.

3 Sian decides to get her book and opens it as well.

4 She writes, as Michael talks to her.

Jonny has assumed the role of a chef as he prepares a pizza for Douglas to eat.

2 He purposefully puts on the oven gloves...

3 ...and opens the oven door. Douglas comes into the kitchen and watches Jonny.

4 Jonny brings out a pizza and shows it to us.

6 He gives Douglas a piece.

7 Douglas sits at the table and presses his fork into the pizza.

8 He raises the fork to his mouth and pretends to eat the pizza.

📽 *Picture story*
PRETEND PLAY (2)
Bringing toys to life – fantasy

When children bring toys to life we are given an insight into their imaginary world. Children change reality by using their imagination, which has no boundaries, and they can become completely absorbed in the activity.

LAURA *3 years 9 months,*
ZAKK *3 years 9 months*

Laura and Zakk have been playing in the play-house for some time. Laura has a toy car, and Zakk has two cows. He can suspend his belief about the role of cows in real life, but Zakk insists that Laura is wrong to assume a car can do the same thing.

Zakk starts the game when he decides to jump outside with his two cows...

3 ...and as Zakk takes the cows off, Laura puts the car on the roof. Zakk says, *'You can't get on the roof.'* Laura says, *'You can.'*

4 Zakk heads for the trees with the cows and places them on a branch. He then says, *'Can't climb up trees.'*

RHIANNA *4 years 6 months* is totally absorbed as she plays with a dolls' house. Rhianna asks the doll where to put the furniture and speaks in a different voice when she replies as the doll.

HAIBATU
3 years 5 months

1 Haibatu is playing with some miniature toy horses. She has carefully selected two yellow ones and one red one.

1 Zakk springs out of the play-house and says, *'Cows they jump in here.'* Laura makes car sounds as she drives it towards Zakk.

2 Zakk then takes the cows and tells Laura, *'Up here on the roof, look.'* Laura nears with the car...

5 Laura puts the car on a branch to show Zakk it can. Zakk says, *'Cars can't.'*

6 As Zakk removes the cows and heads back to the play-house, Laura replies, *'You can, look.'*

2 Haibatu picks up and holds a red and a yellow horse together. She uses a quiet voice to pretend that each horse is talking to the other in turns.

3 As Haibatu plays, she brings her horses to life. She shows that her imagination has no boundaries...

4 ...as her horses fly high above her head, and come together once again.

PRETEND PLAY (3)

Dolls have their own identity

📽️ *Picture story*

KATHERINE *3 years 6 months*

Children are now able to imagine dolls having an identity of their own and that they have emotions that are separate and different from those of the child.

Children will play out real-life situations with a doll, showing they can empathise as well as role-play.

1 Katherine's has named the doll, Dolly. She cuddles Dolly, and gently strokes her head.

2 Katherine decides Dolly needs a nappy change. She begins to undress her.

6 Katherine carefully cleans Dolly...

7 ...then tries to put the nappy on her again.

8 The nappy is too big. Katherine finds Mandy, who helps her put on Dolly's nappy.

12 Katherine scratches her chin as she thinks about how to put the baby-grow on Dolly.

13 Once again, she holds it up, trying to work it out.

14 Eventually she seeks Mandy's help.

Katherine is with Mandy, her child minder. She has borrowed Mandy's daughter's doll with which to play. Immediately, Katherine assumes the role of mother and the doll becomes her baby. She shows that she can order events during an activity, and that she is very patient.

3 When Katherine has finished undressing Dolly, she lies her on top of a new nappy.

4 Katherine then removes it …

5 …as she remembers she has forgotten to use a baby-wipe to clean Dolly first.

9 Katherine returns to the sofa and holds up a baby-grow…

10 …which she attempts to put on Dolly.

11 Katherine finds it difficult and confirms this by her gesture, her arms are out, with her palms upwards.

15 Katherine rolls up Dolly's sleeves…

16 …and zips up the baby-grow.

17 Katherine gently holds Dolly. She has shown empathy, patience and an ability to order events, when being a mother caring for her baby.

📽 *Picture story*
LEARNING BY EXPERIENCE

Children are learning all the time, even if it may not appear obvious to adults. Children are continually exposed to new sensations which we take for granted, but children may not yet have experienced. They also repeat actions to confirm what they anticipate will happen.

CARA 3 *years 1 month*
Cara is waiting for her sister Rhiannon, who is riding. Cara loves small animals, and she has spotted a kitten which she approaches to stroke. Cara shows that she can remember a past experience, when a cat she did not know scratched her.

1 As Cara stokes the kitten, it sniffs the straw on the ground.

HERMIONE 3 *years 11 months*
Hermione has finished an activity and is washing her hands. She has turned the tap on full. As she washes, she becomes fascinated by the way the water flows through her hands.

1 Hermione washes her hands.

2 As she feels the water, she watches as it flows over and through her fingers.

SERINDA 3 *years 1 months*   *Serinda plays with the sand, discovering its properties.*

 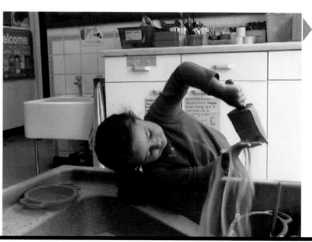

1 Serinda is playing with the sand. She pours the sand from the scoop on to her hand.

2 Serinda leans right over in order to see how the sand looks from this new angle. As she pours out the last of the sand, she opens out her fingers, and watches the sand slip through.

2 The kitten sees a piece of straw move and puts his paw on it. Cara strokes the kitten's paw.

3 The kitten is playful and raises its paw towards Cara's hand, and she immediately removes her hand...

4 ...jumps up and backs away from the kitten. Cara has learned that some cats may scratch, and she shows she can now anticipate when.

3 Hermione makes her hand into a fist, but the water squirts out of the top and sides...

4 ...so she carefully opens out the fingers of her left hand (which she mimics with her right hand), enabling the water to pass through.

5 With great care Hermione closes her finger and thumb together. She has made a circle round the water through which it can flow.

3 Serinda scoops up some more sand...

4 ...and this time leans back, as once more, she observes the sand falling back into the sand-pit.

📽 *Picture story*

READY FOR SCHOOL

Moving forward to the next milestone

The physical, emotional and social skills children have learned during their first years can now be seen coming together. Children can show confidence, patience, co-operation, and have the ability to follow instructions, which, with an eagerness to learn, solve problems and understand how things work, are essential skills to have in place when they start at school.

1 Shenali has icing sugar and butter in the bowl. Carefully, she stirs them together.

5 Shenali takes a spoonful of chocolate icing and places it on the top of the cake.

6 She skilfully begins to spread out the icing.

7 Next, Helen places a bowl of chocolate 'buttons' beside Shenali for her to use when she is ready.

11 Shenali now unscrews the food colouring…

12 …and, encouraged by Helen, she paints a face on her cake.

13 Shenali then breaks a chocolate 'button' in half. She is calm and undisturbed by Haibatu and Serinda as they come close to look.

Nursery teacher, Helen, and the children are going to make chocolate topping, put it on a cake, and add other decorations to make a 'hedgehog'. Shenali shows how skilfully she can complete this task. She further shows she can understand and accept that 'not now' means 'later', and trusts Helen when she says Shenali can eat her cake at milk time. She knows it will happen and willingly gives up her cake..

2 Helen pours some water into the mixture.

3 As Shenali stirs in the water, Helen pours some water into Sydney's bowl, who has been waiting patiently.

4 Shenali has finished mixing and she waits for her turn to be given a cake to decorate.

8 Shenali is unhurried, absorbed in her task.

9 Helen suggests that Shenali leaves some space for the hedgehog's face.

10 Shenali places the spoon back in the icing bowl, indicating she has finished icing.

14 Shenali pushes the two halves of the chocolate 'button' into the icing. Haibatu and Serinda wait patiently for their turn.

15 Shenali checks her work. Helen praises her and says she will put it with Shenali's name. Shenali can eat it at milk time.

16 She gives Helen her cake. Even with the busy goings-on in the nursery Shenali has been able to keep her concentration throughout.

📽 *Every picture tells a story…*

THANK YOU

If we listen we can learn,
When we learn we can understand,
Once we understand we can begin to enjoy…